Hillbilly Elegy and Beyond

J.D. Vance's America in the Age of Trump

Stephanie Johnson

Contents

TIMELINE

1984	Born as James Donald Bowman in Middletown, Ohio.
Late 1980s	Parents divorced, leading to a turbulent home life.
2003	Graduated from Middletown High School.
2004–2007	Served in Iraq as a Marine during the Iraq War.
2007	Returned to the U.S., enrolled at Ohio State University, studying political science and philosophy
2009	Interned at a state senator's office in Ohio.
2010	Graduated summa cum laude from Ohio State University. Accepted into Yale Law School.
2011	Attended a talk by Peter Thiel at Yale, influencing his career and worldview.
2013	Graduated from Yale Law School with a Juris Doctor degree.
2013	Began working as a venture capitalist in Silicon Valley.
2013–2016	Developed an interest in technology, public policy, and cultural issues in the U.S.
2014	Married Usha Chilukuri, whom he met at Yale Law School.
2016	Published *Hillbilly Elegy: A Memoir of a Family and Culture in Crisis*. Criticized Donald Trump during his presidential campaign, calling him "reprehensible."

2017	Relocated to Ohio and founded "Our Ohio Renewal," a nonprofit focused on tackling the opioid epidemic.
2018	Became a contributing editor for *The New York Times*.
2019	Baptized into the Catholic Church, citing the influence of René Girard's philosophy.
2020	The Netflix adaptation of *Hillbilly Elegy*, directed by Ron Howard, was released.
2021	Announced his candidacy for the U.S. Senate seat in Ohio as a Republican.
2022	Elected as the U.S. Senator for Ohio, defeating Democratic opponent Tim Ryan.
2023	Advocated for bipartisan legislation like the Railway Safety Act after the Ohio train derailment and the CHIPS Act, and cosponsored bills on infrastructure, manufacturing, and rail safety
2024	Became Trump's running mate in the presidential race and actively campaigned across the U.S.

INTRODUCTION

In the heartland of America, where steel mills once thrived and working-class dreams were forged, JD Vance's story began. Born into a world of economic decline and familial struggle in Middletown, Ohio, JD rose from humble beginnings to become one of the most polarizing and impactful figures in contemporary American politics. His journey from a troubled Appalachian childhood to a bestselling author, venture capitalist, and U.S. senator encapsulates the complexities of modern America—its fractures, its hopes, and its relentless drive for reinvention.

This biography unpacks the layers of JD's life, tracing the path that brought him from the hardscrabble streets of Ohio to the national stage, where he stands as a symbol of both populist resurgence and conservative transformation. JD's life is not just a personal narrative; it's a lens through which we can explore the broader struggles of a nation grappling with economic shifts, cultural change, and political polarization.

The Roots of Resilience

JD's early years in Middletown were marked by instability. Raised by his grandmother, Mamaw, in the aftermath of his parents' divorce and his mother's battles with addiction, JD found solace in her unyielding belief in hard work and education. Mamaw's no-nonsense approach to life became the bedrock of his values, instilling in him the discipline and grit that would carry him through tumultuous times.

His upbringing reflected the broader challenges faced by Appalachia—a region left reeling from industrial decline and the collapse of traditional family structures. JD's experiences, chronicled in his memoir *Hillbilly Elegy*, resonated deeply with readers across the political spectrum, offering a raw and compassionate look at a community struggling to find its footing in a rapidly changing world. The book became a bestseller, lauded by *The New York Times* as "a compassionate, discerning sociological analysis" and criticized by others for perpetuating stereotypes about the white working class.

From Marine to Yale and Beyond

JD's trajectory took a sharp turn when he joined the U.S. Marine Corps after high school. The military offered him structure and purpose, shaping his outlook on discipline, service, and self-reliance. Serving in Iraq, JD witnessed the complexities of global politics firsthand, experiences that would later inform his views on foreign policy.

After his military service, JD pursued higher education with an intensity that belied his modest beginnings. He graduated from Ohio State University and went on to earn a law degree from Yale. At Yale, JD found himself navigating a world far removed from his Appalachian roots—a world of privilege, opportunity, and, at times, cultural alienation. It was here that he began to articulate the chasm between the America he grew up in and the one he now inhabited.

The Making of a Conservative Voice

JD's political identity evolved significantly over the years. In 2016, during Donald Trump's first presidential campaign, JD was a vocal critic of Trump's rhetoric, describing him as "reprehensible." Yet, as the political landscape shifted, so did JD's perspective. By 2020, he had become an ardent supporter of Trump, aligning himself with the former president's populist agenda. This transformation—from skeptic to ally—marked one of the most dramatic pivots in modern conservative politics.

Critics accused JD of opportunism, while supporters saw a man unafraid to change his mind in the face of new realities. JD himself described the shift as a recognition of the failures of both political parties to address the needs of working-class Americans. His critique of the political and economic establishment resonated with voters who felt left behind, cementing his place as a leading voice in the conservative movement.

The Leap Into Politics

In 2022, JD ran for the U.S. Senate, representing Ohio. His campaign was emblematic of the new Republican Party—a coalition of cultural conservatives, economic populists, and Trump loyalists. JD's platform focused on issues like border security, economic revitalization, and combating the influence of "woke" ideologies in education and business.

JD's Senate bid drew national attention, not only for his high-profile endorsements but also for his controversial statements on topics ranging from immigration to cultural values. These remarks often sparked outrage but also galvanized his base, who saw him as a fearless truth-teller in an era of political correctness.

Culture Wars and Legislative Ambitions

As a senator, JD quickly made his mark, championing legislation on issues like corporate accountability, immigration reform, and the opioid crisis. His cultural critiques—asserting that "the culture war is class war"—reflected his belief that progressive ideologies were eroding the values of middle America.

JD's legislative record showcased his commitment to reshoring American manufacturing and reducing dependency on foreign powers like China. At the same time, his proposals, such as criminalizing gender-affirming care for minors and cracking down on affirmative action, placed him at the center of America's culture wars. Supporters hailed these efforts as necessary corrections to societal overreach; detractors decried them as divisive and regressive.

A Polarizing Figure

JD's rise has been anything but uncontroversial. His comments about childless leaders and cultural elites drew widespread criticism, as did his unsubstantiated claims about immigrant communities. Yet, these controversies only seemed to solidify his standing among his supporters, who viewed him as a champion of free speech and a defender of traditional values.

In his public statements, JD often emphasized his loyalty to the working class, contrasting his own modest upbringing with the privileges of America's political and economic elite. He framed his politics as a rejection of technocratic solutions in favor of grassroots empowerment, appealing to voters who felt disillusioned by decades of bipartisan failure.

Legacy and Impact

Whether celebrated as a principled conservative or criticized as a polarizing opportunist, JD's impact on American politics is undeniable. His life story—one of resilience, reinvention, and relentless ambition—mirrors the broader struggles and aspirations of a nation in flux. Through his writing, speeches, and political career, JD has positioned himself as a voice for those who feel unheard, a champion of populist ideals, and a lightning rod for controversy.

As this biography unfolds, it will explore the complexities of JD's journey, offering a deeper understanding of the man behind the headlines. From his Appalachian roots to his role on the national stage, JD's story is a testament to the enduring power of personal transformation—and the challenges of navigating an increasingly polarized political landscape.

CHILDHOOD

*'Americans call them hillbillies, rednecks, or white trash.
I call them neighbors, friends, and family.'*

CHAPTER 1

A Hillbilly's Journey

JD's early life revolved around two contrasting worlds—Ohio and the Appalachian town of Jackson, Kentucky. While he lived in Ohio with his mother, he considered his true home to be the holler in Jackson, where his great-grandmother lived. Jackson, a small town in southeastern Kentucky, represented warmth, family, and belonging. Its community upheld traditions like standing at attention for funeral motorcades, a reflection of their deep respect for others.

JD spent summers and holidays in Jackson with his grandmother, Mamaw. The holler's simplicity and natural beauty fascinated him as a child. He and his cousins roamed the mountains, catching animals and playing until they were scolded into bed. Despite the charm of Jackson, poverty was ever-present. Many families, including his, struggled with financial hardships, but Mamaw shielded him from much of the harshness.

His maternal family, the Blantons, were larger-than-life figures. They represented a mix of rugged justice, Appalachian honor, and unchecked temper. Uncle Pet, for instance, beat a man nearly to death over an insult to his mother, while Uncle Teaberry once forced someone to eat his sister's underwear for making a vulgar comment. These men symbolized hillbilly resilience but also carried vices—anger, neglect, and violence. To JD, they were heroes, embodying the spirit of his roots.

However, Jackson was far from idyllic. The town was plagued by poverty, substance abuse, and failing schools. Many families, including JD's, migrated to places like Middletown, Ohio, in search of better opportunities. Yet, the issues of Appalachia—addiction, poor health, and fractured families—followed them. His mother battled drug addiction, and JD had to adapt to a revolving door of father figures. Each man brought new challenges, yet none filled the void of stability.

Despite these struggles, his grandmother Mamaw remained a constant in his life. Fierce, loyal, and protective, she instilled in him the values of hard work and perseverance. Mamaw's tough love and unflinching honesty guided JD through his turbulent upbringing. She was a force of nature, determined to shield him from the chaos around them.

As JD grew older, he saw the contradictions of Jackson more clearly. The town was beautiful but marred by environmental neglect. Its people were kind yet burdened by addiction and poverty. While he cherished his roots, he recognized the darker realities of his heritage.

Visiting Jackson as an adult, JD saw how the town had deteriorated. Drug addiction and economic decline had taken a toll. Once-safe neighborhoods were now dangerous, and opportunities were scarce. Yet, these struggles were not confined to Appalachia. The migration of hill people to cities like Middletown spread their challenges across the Midwest, creating what JD calls "Middletucky."

Roots and Resilience

JD's grandparents, Mamaw and Papaw, were central to his life. They provided him with love, stability, and the lessons he needed to believe in the American Dream. Born into Appalachian poverty, both grandparents grew up in the harsh, isolated hills of Kentucky. Their early years shaped their tough personalities and deep loyalty to family.

Papaw, born in 1929, was raised by his strict grandfather after his father's death and his mother's absence. He grew up near the Blantons, a family known for their fierce tempers and feuding. Papaw became an honorary Blanton, spending much of his youth with them. Eventually, he married Bonnie Blanton, later known as Mamaw, a fiery teenager from a family of proud hillbillies.

Their marriage began dramatically. At just thirteen and sixteen, Mamaw and Papaw left Jackson for Ohio under the pressure of Mamaw's pregnancy, which tragically ended with the baby's death. Seeking a better life, they settled in Middletown, where Papaw found work at the steel company Armco, part of a larger migration of Appalachian families to industrial towns in the Midwest.

Life in Middletown was a mix of opportunity and struggle. Papaw and Mamaw worked hard to adapt to their new environment while staying connected to their Appalachian roots. The community in Middletown was filled with other hillbilly transplants, but the cultural clash between their old ways and the expectations of their new life was difficult. Neighbors viewed them with suspicion, and their own family back in Kentucky accused them of abandoning their roots.

Mamaw, fiercely protective of her family, struggled with isolation. She longed for the extended family support system she had in Jackson.

She also had dreams of becoming a children's attorney but lacked the resources and opportunities to pursue them. Despite these limitations, Mamaw devoted herself to helping others, especially children, and instilled in her family the value of hard work and resilience.

Papaw, a steady provider, believed in the promise of the American Dream but knew the road was hard. He and Mamaw raised their children with the hope that they would succeed beyond what was possible in Kentucky. However, their children faced challenges of their own, grappling with the cultural and social disconnection of growing up far from their Appalachian roots.

A Family in Turmoil and Transformation

JD's grandparents, Mamaw and Papaw, had three children—Jimmy, Bev (JD's mother), and Lori. Their early years as parents were marked by struggle and heartbreak. Mamaw endured nine miscarriages before giving birth to Bev and Lori, carrying emotional scars that shaped her outlook on life. Despite these challenges, the family settled into a seemingly middle-class life in Middletown, Ohio, with a suburban home and steady income from Papaw's job at Armco.

Jimmy, the eldest, recalled a brief period of family unity when life seemed "normal." Yet, as Papaw's drinking worsened and Mamaw became increasingly reclusive, the veneer of stability crumbled. Mamaw's hoarding tendencies escalated, and her fiery personality alienated neighbors. Papaw's behavior, fueled by alcohol, often brought chaos. On bad days, he would return home drunk, causing fights that left lasting impressions on their children. One Christmas Eve, he drunkenly threw the family's Christmas tree out the door. On another occasion, a fight with Mamaw ended with her throwing a vase at Papaw, splitting his forehead.

Mamaw, though sober, was equally volatile. She retaliated against Papaw's drinking by sabotaging his clothes, hiding his wallet, and even setting him on fire when he passed out drunk. Despite these violent episodes, their marriage endured, albeit with constant tension. Mamaw often expressed her frustrations with biting humor, calling herself a "crazy bitch" while fiercely demanding loyalty from her family.

The children bore the brunt of their parents' dysfunctional marriage. Jimmy escaped by moving out at eighteen and taking a job at Armco, despite Papaw's hopes that he would pursue higher education. Lori, nicknamed Aunt Wee, struggled with school attendance and dropped out at sixteen. She married young but found herself trapped in an abusive relationship, echoing the instability of her childhood. Eventually, Lori turned her life around, finding stability in a second marriage and a career in radiology.

Bev, JD's mother, faced even greater challenges. A promising student, she became pregnant at eighteen and married her boyfriend. The marriage quickly fell apart, leaving her a single mother to JD's older sister, Lindsay. Bev's life spiraled into a cycle of poor decisions, failed relationships, and struggles with addiction. She seemed unable to escape the chaos that had defined her upbringing.

Despite their tumultuous marriage, Mamaw and Papaw worked to support their children and grandchildren. Papaw quit drinking in 1983, ending decades of turmoil. Though they separated, Mamaw and Papaw reconciled and spent most of their time together, living in separate houses but maintaining a close bond. They helped Lori leave her abusive marriage, provided financial and emotional support to Bev, and stepped in as surrogate parents when Bev faltered.

Mamaw and Papaw's later years were marked by a sense of redemption. They tried to make amends for the mistakes of their past by creating a more stable environment for their grandchildren. Through their resilience and efforts, they became a vital source of love and stability in JD's life, offering him a path forward despite the challenges of his family's history.

CHAPTER 2

Born into Decline

JD was born in late summer 1984, a time of significant change for both his family and the country. His grandfather, Papaw, cast his only Republican vote that year, supporting Ronald Reagan over Walter Mondale. This act symbolized the cultural disconnect between working-class hillbillies like Papaw and the political elite. While Papaw's loyalty remained with the "party of the workingman," his vote for Reagan marked a moment of frustration with the direction of the Democratic Party.

JD was born and raised in Middletown, Ohio, a Rust Belt town shaped by the migration of Appalachian families like his grandparents decades earlier. Though Middletown retained a surface stability when JD was young, the undercurrents of economic and social decline were already evident. The town, once a thriving manufacturing hub, began losing its luster. Jobs at Armco Steel, the economic backbone of Middletown, were under threat as globalization reshaped industries. Despite this, Papaw often remarked that "Armco built this town," a testament to its influence on the community and its people.

Middletown's decline mirrored broader trends in Rust Belt towns. Once-proud neighborhoods deteriorated as poverty crept in. JD grew up in a socioeconomically mixed environment, with wealthy areas near the high school contrasting starkly with neighborhoods near the steel mills, where poverty was most visible. JD's own neighborhood, with single-family homes near abandoned factories, sat somewhere in between. The gradual erosion of public spaces, like Miami Park across from his house, symbolized this decline. What was once a vibrant community park became overgrown and neglected, a reflection of the town's dwindling resources and care.

As Middletown changed, so did its people. The cultural values of the Appalachian migrants who had built the town persisted but began to clash with the harsh realities of economic hardship. JD's family, deeply rooted in these values, embodied this tension. They held onto ideals of hard work, loyalty, and resilience, but the socioeconomic shifts created strains that were difficult to overcome.

The merger of Armco Steel with Kawasaki in 1989 highlighted the challenges of globalization. While the merger saved the company and many local jobs, it also symbolized the uneasy adaptation to a changing world. Papaw, initially resistant to the idea of a Japanese company taking part in Middletown's legacy, eventually accepted the reality, remarking that "the Japanese are our friends now." This pragmatism underscored the community's struggle to balance pride in its heritage with the need to survive in a globalized economy.

JD's early life in Middletown was shaped by the dichotomy between its fading past and uncertain future. The town's decline paralleled the challenges facing his family and the broader Appalachian culture. The ideals of self-reliance and resilience, central themes in JD's life, were tested by the realities of economic dislocation, cultural decay, and the fraying social fabric.

A Town of Contradictions

JD was born into a Middletown, Ohio, that still bore the marks of its industrial heyday. The steel mill, Armco, remained a source of pride, providing stable jobs, funding parks, and symbolizing the American Dream for the blue-collar workers who depended on it. Papaw, JD's grandfather, retired from Armco with a pension and stock, representing a generation that had climbed into the middle class through hard work in the mills. Yet, the foundations of this dream were beginning to erode by the time JD was born.

As a child, JD and his peers grew up blissfully unaware of the changes underway. The town's decline was gradual, more erosion than collapse, and many families maintained a sense of normalcy. At school, kids dreamt of becoming astronauts, doctors, or businesspeople—rarely steelworkers. The mill jobs, once the backbone of the community, were taken for granted. Even as economic opportunities began dwindling, there was a collective ignorance about how the world outside Middletown was shifting.

This disconnect wasn't unique to JD's generation. His grandparents saw Armco as a savior, lifting them from the poverty of Jackson, Kentucky. Papaw, deeply proud of the mill's legacy, knew every car model made with Armco steel. Yet, he discouraged JD from following in his footsteps. "Your generation will make its living with their minds, not their hands," he told him. Moving up meant moving on, and for JD, that required education—a path the family had little experience navigating.

Despite this aspiration, barriers to higher education were omnipresent in Middletown. Few families had members who had gone to college, and success often seemed like a matter of luck or innate talent rather than hard work. Teachers and parents rarely pushed students to excel, fostering an unspoken belief that mediocrity was acceptable. JD absorbed this atmosphere, seeing his classmates and neighbors aim low or avoid ambition altogether. Some assumed they could follow their relatives into dwindling mill jobs, while others clung to unrealistic dreams without taking the steps to achieve them.

For JD, the contradictions of his environment were stark. Middletown prided itself on hard work, yet many residents worked few hours or relied on welfare. Ambition was discussed, but it wasn't modeled consistently. At school, moments of realization about his own gaps in knowledge, such as discovering multiplication for the first time, left him feeling inadequate. However, these moments also fueled his determination.

At home, JD received a different message. Papaw, despite his rough edges, took an active role in JD's education. When JD struggled with math, Papaw turned it into an opportunity, teaching him multiplication and division in a single evening. These weekly math lessons, reinforced with rewards like ice cream, instilled a sense of resilience and self-improvement in JD. His mother, though inconsistent in many areas, ensured he had access to books and encouraged his love of learning.

These small interventions made all the difference. In a town where stagnation seemed inevitable, JD's family gave him the tools to break free. Papaw's belief in education and his relentless encouragement showed JD that he didn't have to accept the limitations of his surroundings. Despite the decay of Middletown and the cultural barriers that discouraged ambition, JD found a path forward, rooted in the values of perseverance and self-reliance that his family embodied.

CHAPTER 3

Lessons of Loyalty, Education, and Strength

JD's early childhood was marked by a blend of chaos, love, and foundational lessons that would shape his future. Born in 1984, JD's first memories reflect the quirks of his family and the contradictions of his environment. His upbringing in Middletown, Ohio, an industrial town in decline, mirrored his family's struggles with identity, class, and ambition. These early years, filled with both joy and hardship, introduced themes of loyalty, resilience, and the transformative power of education.

JD's biological father, Don Bowman, was a fleeting figure in his life. By the time JD was six, his father had given him up for adoption. JD was told he had been "replaced" by his father's new family, a revelation that left him heartbroken. This absence was filled by Bob Hamel, JD's stepfather and later adoptive father. Bob, a truck driver with rotting teeth and a penchant for Mountain Dew, embodied the hillbilly stereotype that JD's grandmother, Mamaw, despised. Mamaw's disdain for Bob was rooted not just in his character but in her aspirations for her children and grandchildren to transcend their Appalachian roots.

Mamaw's influence loomed large over JD's childhood. Despite her own flaws, she was fiercely loyal and determined to instill values of toughness and honor in her grandchildren. She taught JD how to fight, not just physically but also for what was right. When JD stood up to a class bully in third grade, delivering a swift punch to the stomach, Mamaw praised him for defending a weaker child. This moment epitomized the unspoken code of loyalty and justice she imparted—a code that often clashed with societal norms but carried deep personal meaning.

Fighting was not just about physical strength; it was a metaphor for survival in a harsh world. Mamaw's lessons extended beyond the playground, teaching JD to stand tall in the face of adversity. However, her views evolved over time. She began to discourage unnecessary fights, emphasizing that strength lay in knowing when to walk away. These lessons of measured aggression and standing up for others became part of JD's moral framework.

Amid the chaos of his family life, education emerged as a beacon of hope and possibility. JD's mother, Bev, despite her struggles, valued learning deeply. She was the salutatorian of her high school but had abandoned her college ambitions after becoming a young mother. Later, she earned a nursing degree and encouraged JD's intellectual curiosity. From football strategies to science fair projects, Bev supported JD's academic endeavors, sometimes to an excessive degree—such as redoing his entire science project overnight, a move that backfired when judges realized the mismatch between the presentation and JD's knowledge.

Papaw, JD's grandfather, also played a crucial role in fostering his intellectual growth. When JD struggled with math, Papaw patiently taught him multiplication and division, turning it into a bonding ritual with rewards like ice cream. These moments underscored the importance of persistence and the belief that intelligence could be cultivated through effort.

Despite this support, the broader environment in Middletown often conveyed a different message. Many in JD's community viewed success as either a matter of luck or innate talent. Hard work was valued in theory, but the town's economic decline and limited opportunities created a pervasive sense of stagnation. Students at JD's school rarely aspired to attend college, let alone succeed beyond their parents' achievements. This cultural inertia contrasted sharply with the values Mamaw and Papaw tried to instill in JD, encouraging him to aim higher.

Loyalty was another recurring theme in JD's life, shaping his relationships and worldview. Mamaw's unwavering loyalty to her family often manifested in blunt and unconventional ways. She taught JD to prioritize family above all else, reinforcing the idea that his sister Lindsay was his "only true friend" and that family bonds were sacred. Even her harsh criticisms of JD's stepfather Bob stemmed from a desire to protect her grandchildren and push them toward better lives.

Yet, loyalty was not blind acceptance. Mamaw's sense of honor demanded standing up against injustice, even within the family. When JD felt guilty for not defending a classmate from a bully, Mamaw encouraged him to act the next day, teaching him that sometimes fighting for what is right is necessary. These lessons of loyalty and justice extended beyond personal conflicts, shaping JD's understanding of responsibility and morality.

Throughout these formative years, JD's family struggled with the same contradictions that defined their community. Middletown, once a thriving industrial town, was in decline, its values of hard work and community eroded by economic hardship and cultural shifts. Mamaw and Papaw represented a generation that had clawed its way into the middle class through sheer determination. They expected JD to continue this upward trajectory, believing education was the key to a better life.

However, the path was not always clear. JD often felt the weight of his environment's limitations, from teachers who underestimated students to a culture that seemed resigned to mediocrity. Yet, his family's unwavering belief in his potential provided a counterbalance. Papaw's pride in teaching JD math and Mamaw's insistence on standing up for himself and others instilled in him the resilience to rise above his circumstances.

By the time JD reached adolescence, the lessons of his early years had begun to crystallize. His family's struggles, from his mother's erratic parenting to his stepfather's flaws, were tempered by the support and values Mamaw and Papaw provided. Their belief in the transformative power of education and their fierce loyalty gave JD a foundation to navigate the challenges of his upbringing.

JD's childhood was a microcosm of the larger story of working-class America—a tale of contradictions, resilience, and hope. His early experiences in Middletown shaped his understanding of the world and set the stage for his journey to overcome the challenges of his environment. Themes of loyalty, education, and strength ran through these years, preparing JD to navigate a life that would test his resolve and push him toward a brighter future.

CHAPTER 4

Chaos, Conflict, and the Struggle for Stability

JD's childhood was shaped by constant chaos, family conflict, and fleeting stability. Raised in a chaotic household, JD witnessed intense fights between his mother, Bev, and stepfather, Bob. These battles often turned physical, leaving JD in a state of anxiety and turmoil. Despite the dysfunction, JD found moments of happiness within the extended family dynamic typical of Appalachian culture, where grandparents, aunts, uncles, and cousins all played significant roles.

When JD was nine, his life began to unravel further. His family moved from Middletown, Ohio, to rural Preble County, isolating him from the safety net of his grandparents, Mamaw and Papaw. Mamaw, a fiercely protective and fiery figure, had been JD's anchor. She provided discipline, comfort, and a sense of security in a world that often felt unstable. Her absence was deeply felt as tensions between Bev and Bob escalated in the new home.

Bev's marriage to Bob, her third husband, deteriorated quickly. Their arguments, initially verbal, turned violent. JD vividly recalls one night when he intervened during a fight, punching Bob to protect his mother. Though Bob never retaliated, the incident left JD shaken and fearful. The constant fighting at home affected JD's school performance, his grades slipping as he struggled to concentrate amid sleepless nights filled with yelling and breaking furniture.

Financial strain further compounded the family's troubles, despite Bev and Bob earning a combined income of over $100,000. They spent recklessly on unnecessary luxuries, including new cars and a swimming pool, accumulating significant debt with little to show for it. The financial instability mirrored the emotional chaos, leaving JD with no sense of stability or peace.

Amid the dysfunction, Mamaw remained a crucial influence, offering JD lessons on loyalty and resilience. When a bully targeted a vulnerable classmate, Mamaw encouraged JD to stand up for the boy, even if it meant physical confrontation. She taught JD that fighting was sometimes necessary to defend what was right, reinforcing a moral code of standing up for others.

Eventually, Bev and Bob's volatile marriage ended after a particularly dramatic confrontation. Bev had been involved in a years-long affair with a local fireman, and when Bob discovered it, the ensuing argument drove her to a suicide attempt—or what Mamaw believed was a manipulative act to divert attention from her actions. Bev intentionally crashed her car into a telephone pole but survived with minor injuries. The family soon moved back to Middletown, leaving Bob behind.

Returning to Middletown brought JD closer to Mamaw and Papaw, but it did little to stabilize Bev's behavior. Her erratic actions intensified; she cycled through boyfriends, partied late into the night, and became increasingly detached from her role as a mother. JD and his sister Lindsay were left to navigate the turbulence on their own, with Mamaw providing occasional refuge.

The chaos of JD's home life took a toll on his physical and emotional health. He began gaining weight and often complained of stomachaches, symptoms of the stress he endured. The constant upheaval left him feeling trapped, longing for silence and stability. Yet, he found himself drawn to the drama, observing fights with a mix of fear and fascination.

A Tumultuous Childhood and the Search for Belonging

One incident stands out as a turning point in his young life. After a heated argument, Bev threatened to crash their car and kill them both. Terrified, JD leapt into the backseat and tried to secure himself with multiple seatbelts. Furious, Bev stopped the car and attempted to physically assault him. JD managed to escape and ran through a field to seek refuge in a stranger's home. The homeowner, though initially supportive, stood by helplessly as Bev broke down the door and dragged JD out. Fortunately, police arrived in time to arrest Bev and take her away.

This incident was the culmination of years of tension and instability. JD found solace with his grandparents, Mamaw and Papaw, who had always provided him with a sense of safety and consistency. After Bev's arrest, Mamaw assured JD he could live with her whenever he chose. This marked a turning point in his life, as Mamaw's house became his true home, even though Bev retained legal custody.

Mamaw's fierce love and "hillbilly justice" were defining features of JD's upbringing. She promised to protect him at all costs, even threatening violence if Bev tried to interfere. This fierce loyalty shaped JD's values and gave him a sense of security in an otherwise chaotic world. Papaw, though often stoic, showed rare moments of vulnerability, such as the time he broke down in tears after the ordeal with Bev. These moments reinforced JD's belief in the unconditional love of his grandparents.

Despite the safety Mamaw and Papaw provided, JD couldn't escape the broader challenges of his environment. Growing up in Middletown, Ohio, he saw firsthand the struggles of working-class families. His experiences in court after Bev's arrest highlighted the class divide. The judges, lawyers, and social workers spoke in polished "TV accents," starkly contrasting with the sweatpants and frizzy-haired parents in the courtroom. JD recognized these people as kin—part of the same struggling Appalachian community his family had been a part of for generations.

A trip to California provided JD with a broader perspective. Visiting his uncle Jimmy in Napa, JD experienced a world far removed from the economic struggles of Ohio. The cultural differences were striking, but the journey helped him understand his roots more deeply. People in California thought JD's accent sounded "Kentucky," a reflection of his hillbilly heritage. Despite the adventure, he realized that most of his life had been spent in places where people shared his background, values, and struggles.

CHAPTER 5

Faith, Family, and His Sister Lindsay

JD's relationship with his sister Lindsay was one of the most defining aspects of his early life. Despite their chaotic upbringing, Lindsay was his unwavering protector and caretaker. She wasn't just his older sister; she was his "whole sister," a term he used with pride. When JD learned that Lindsay was technically his "half-sister" because they had different fathers, he was devastated. Mamaw's casual explanation of the term led JD to scream in anguish, and he only calmed down after Mamaw promised never to use "half-sister" again. To JD, Lindsay was his anchor in a stormy sea.

Lindsay was five years older than JD, but she carried the responsibilities of an adult long before her time. She often stepped in when their mother's instability disrupted their lives. When their mother left JD in an empty parking lot to teach Lindsay a lesson during a fight, it was Lindsay's grief and rage that forced their mother to return. In times of crisis, Lindsay called Mamaw and Papaw to intervene, shielding JD as best as she could from their mother's explosive fights. She cooked meals, did laundry, and cared for JD with a maturity far beyond her years. To JD, Lindsay wasn't just a sibling—she was a hero.

One pivotal moment in their relationship came when the family decided to support Lindsay's dream of becoming a model. JD idolized her, ranking her above celebrities like Demi Moore and Pam Anderson. At a modeling audition in Dayton, both Lindsay and JD were selected for a second round in New York City. Excitement filled the car as they imagined their futures. But the dream quickly unraveled when their mother began worrying about the cost of the trip. The car ride turned into a violent argument, with shouting and slapping in the backseat. Mamaw intervened, threatening their mother to ensure they made it home safely. That night, JD saw Lindsay's heartbreak as she retreated to bed, her dream shattered.

Amid the chaos, JD grappled with deeper questions about faith. That night, standing in Mamaw's house, he asked her if God loved them. The question brought Mamaw to tears, revealing her own struggles with faith in the face of their hardships. Despite not attending church regularly, Mamaw's deeply personal and unconventional faith shaped the family. She despised organized religion but maintained a strong belief in God, often supporting small churches in her hometown.

JD's understanding of faith was shaped by his Mamaw's earthy, practical theology. She believed God was always present, offering guidance and support, but emphasized personal responsibility with her favorite parable: God helps those who help themselves. Her faith provided JD with lessons in perseverance, forgiveness, and the importance of hard work. Amid the chaos of his upbringing, JD sought reassurance that God loved them, yearning for deeper meaning in their struggles. Mamaw's belief in a divine plan and justice helped JD make sense of a turbulent world filled with both heartache and hope.

JD Vance's childhood was marked by a revolving door of father figures, each bringing a wave of hope followed by disappointment. His mother, driven by a mix of love, guilt, and her own need for companionship, constantly sought out men to fill the paternal void in her children's lives. She often justified these relationships by pointing out the benefits they offered to JD and his sister Lindsay—whether it was learning masculinity or gaining a stable male presence. But her efforts were often short-lived and chaotic, leaving JD to navigate the emotional turbulence of men entering and exiting their lives.

Bob, one of these figures, was legally JD's father after adopting him, but his departure mirrored the fate of many who came before. JD didn't mourn Bob's absence as much as he feared the disruption it would cause. His childhood was already defined by instability, and each breakup reinforced a harsh truth: the people meant to provide stability often disappeared instead.

This cycle of attachment and loss shaped JD's worldview. He learned to distrust permanence, understanding from a young age that men in his life could leave without warning. Lindsay, older and more skeptical, had already adopted this view, and with Bob's departure, JD followed suit. The siblings bonded through shared experiences, with Lindsay acting as a protector and surrogate parent. Her resilience during their mother's turbulent relationships often shielded JD from their worst effects.

When his biological father, Don Bowman, re-entered JD's life, it brought a mix of curiosity and hope. Don's life was markedly different from the chaos JD had known. On his farm, JD experienced peace and simplicity—a far cry from his mother's tumultuous home. Don's household was calm, structured, and filled with love, even if it lacked some of the indulgences JD was used to. The contrast between his two worlds highlighted the themes of identity and belonging that permeated JD's life.

At Don's farm, JD felt connected to his Kentucky roots, finding solace in the land, animals, and familial routines that mirrored his visits to Mamaw's home. For the first time, he experienced what a stable, loving household could look like, free from screaming matches and chaos. This brief exposure to serenity stayed with JD, influencing his understanding of family, masculinity, and what it meant to build a life filled with purpose and care.

CHAPTER 6

Faith, Fatherhood, and the Search for Stability

JD Vance's relationship with his father, Don Bowman, and his introduction to Bowman's church marked a significant chapter in his life, one shaped by themes of redemption, religious influence, and the search for stability amidst chaos. His father, absent during JD's formative years, re-entered his life a changed man, attributing his transformation to a deeper commitment to his faith. This change starkly contrasted with JD's previous understanding of his father, colored by accounts of anger and aggression from his mother and family.

Bowman's faith-centered lifestyle introduced JD to a structured, supportive community unlike the tumultuous environment he experienced with his mother. His father's church offered tangible benefits—assistance with addiction, parenting, and financial troubles—that mirrored what the broken world around them desperately needed. These positive influences created a compelling draw for JD, especially as his father shared stories of his efforts to retain custody and his ultimate decision to relinquish JD for what he believed was his son's best interest. Though JD struggled with the pain of abandonment, learning his father's perspective eased some of the resentment he carried.

Religion became both a refuge and a source of tension for JD Under his father's guidance, he immersed himself in evangelical teachings, embracing its rules and beliefs with fervor. The church's strict moral framework and emphasis on cultural battles, however, introduced new conflicts. JD found himself questioning mainstream science, viewing secular influences with suspicion, and embracing apocalyptic narratives. These teachings, while appealing in their simplicity, also distanced him from broader perspectives and created tensions with loved ones, including his Catholic uncle Dan and even Mamaw, whose unconventional yet heartfelt faith stood apart from the dogma of JD's church.

Amidst this tension, JD grappled with questions of identity and morality. His encounter with a fire-and-brimstone sermon led him to momentarily fear he was destined for hell, a misunderstanding resolved with Mamaw's unfiltered pragmatism and her reassurance of unconditional love. This episode highlighted the gap between the fear-based teachings of his church and Mamaw's approach, which prioritized compassion over condemnation.

While JD appreciated the structure and support the church provided, its rigid worldview planted the seeds for his later disillusionment with evangelicalism. Nonetheless, the church offered him and his father a shared purpose, strengthening their bond during a time when JD desperately needed both a paternal figure and a sense of belonging.

A Turning Point

At thirteen, JD faced one of the greatest losses of his life: the sudden death of his grandfather, Papaw. It was an ordinary evening when Mamaw's worried call shattered the calm. Papaw, known for his predictable routine, had vanished from his daily rhythm—no visit to Mamaw, no McDonald's coffee with old friends, no farewell before evening. JD, sensing the worst, broke down in tears as his mother arrived home. Together, they rushed to Papaw's house, only to confirm their fears. He had passed away, hunched in his chair, leaving an indelible void in their lives.

For JD and his family, Papaw was more than a grandfather—he was a pillar of stability. Despite his gruff demeanor, he embodied love and reliability, values that had been scarce in JD's tumultuous childhood. Lindsay, JD's sister, shared a deep bond with Papaw, though teenage distractions sometimes obscured her appreciation. When she learned of his passing, her grief was marked by regret, reflecting on how much she had relied on him without fully expressing her gratitude.

This event underscored a recurring theme in JD's life: the fear of imposing on others. Both he and Lindsay had learned to navigate relationships cautiously, wary of overburdening those they depended on. Yet, Papaw had been an exception. His presence allowed them to feel secure, even in moments of chaos. His death magnified their sense of vulnerability, as JD and Lindsay grappled with the idea that no one else could offer the same unconditional support.

Papaw's passing also highlighted the divide between the family's roots in Jackson, Kentucky, and their life in Ohio. Even in death, his dual identity was evident, with visitations held in both locations. For JD, this split mirrored his own internal conflict—a longing for the simplicity and loyalty of his Appalachian heritage, tempered by the challenges of carving a path in a new world.

On the morning after Papaw's death, as Lynyrd Skynyrd's "Tuesday's Gone" played on the radio, JD grasped the permanence of his loss. It was a moment of profound clarity, as he realized Papaw's influence would forever shape his life.

At Papaw's funeral in Jackson, JD faced the immense weight of loss alongside his family. The gathering brought together uncles, cousins, and old friends, many of whom JD had seen only at funerals in recent years. As he sat among the mourners, memories of Papaw's larger-than-life presence filled his mind, from their quiet moments together to the legendary stories that defined his grandfather's grit and humor.

Papaw had been a cornerstone in JD's life, stepping into the role of father figure with a mix of tough love and tenderness. JD recalled how Papaw had taught him life skills like shooting a BB gun, aligning its scope with precision, lessons that later helped JD excel in Marine Corps marksmanship. Papaw's gruff demeanor—punctuated by his signature "Bullshit!"—belied a deep affection for his family, evident in how he spoiled JD and Lindsay with small acts of love, like fixing up cars for Lindsay after each accident.

Hillbilly funerals, as JD observed, often reflected the chaos and humor of the lives being mourned. Papaw's was no exception. JD thought back to an earlier funeral, where Mamaw and Papaw had barricaded the exits with loaded guns, convinced a child predator had taken him when, in reality, he was asleep in a church pew. That story, like so many others, illustrated Papaw's fierce protectiveness—a trait that defined his love.

Papaw's wisdom often came through action rather than words. He showed JD how intelligence was not innate but earned through effort and patience. He modeled resilience and loyalty, despite his own earlier failures. Papaw's rough edges never masked his belief that a man's character was measured by how he treated the women in his life—a lesson JD carried with him.

When JD stood to speak at the funeral, he expressed the essence of Papaw's influence: "I never had a dad, but Papaw was always there for me. He was the best dad anyone could ever ask for." Those words summed up a lifetime of guidance and unconditional love.

CHAPTER 7

A Family's Struggle with Addiction and Recovery

After Papaw's death, the cracks in JD Vance's family became impossible to ignore, with his mother's descent into addiction pushing the family into uncharted territory. JD's narrative reveals the profound impact of addiction, loss, and resilience on their lives as they grappled with recovery and rebuilding relationships.

Papaw's passing brought grief that manifested differently for everyone. For JD's mother, Bev, the loss spiraled into a crisis that had been brewing for years. Her grief turned explosive, with outbursts that alienated her family and left her vulnerable. Her public breakdown—a chaotic scene involving the police and threats of self-harm—marked the tipping point that led her to rehab at the Cincinnati Center for Addiction Treatment, or the "CAT house."

JD, only 13 at the time, found himself navigating a new reality. With Bev in rehab, JD and his sister Lindsay relied on each other for stability. Lindsay, just out of high school, became the de facto adult in their lives, balancing her own struggles with the responsibility of caring for JD Together, they forged a routine, cooking simple meals and fending for themselves, while Mamaw provided support from a distance.

Visits to the rehab center exposed JD to the harsh realities of addiction. Wednesdays were spent in group sessions where families confronted raw emotions and old wounds. For JD, these sessions were a revelation, allowing him to witness Lindsay's courage as she confronted their mother. In these moments, JD began to see his sister as the true adult in the family—a stabilizing force amid chaos.

Rehab gave Bev a new vocabulary and purpose. She adopted the language of recovery, reciting the Serenity Prayer and framing her addiction as a disease. While JD found this perspective difficult to accept, he recognized her effort and joined her Narcotics Anonymous meetings in a show of support. These meetings offered a window into the lives of others battling addiction, including one man whose roots traced back to the same hills of eastern Kentucky as JD's grandparents.

Through it all, JD and Lindsay developed a quiet resilience. They learned to navigate crises together, drawing strength from each other and from the legacy of their grandparents.

A Summer of Change:
Balancing Family, Identity, and Belonging

As JD prepared for high school, life seemed momentarily stable. His mother, Bev, had been sober for over a year, and her relationship with Matt had lasted long enough to offer some consistency. His sister Lindsay had started her own family, giving birth to her son Kameron, and JD took pride in his new role as an uncle. Even Mamaw seemed to find some peace, taking vacations to visit family in California and to Las Vegas with a friend. These signs of renewal gave JD hope for the future.

That summer, however, Bev announced a plan that threatened JD's fragile sense of stability. She wanted him to move to Dayton and live with Matt, who had his own home there. This meant leaving Middletown, his school, friends, and the comforting proximity of Mamaw, who had always been his safety net. For JD, the move symbolized a return to instability, where familiar support systems would no longer be within reach. He refused, sparking a battle of wills between him and his mother.

In response, Bev involved her therapist, scheduling a session for JD to address what she perceived as his "anger problems." The meeting felt like an ambush. The therapist, relying heavily on Bev's accounts, confronted JD with allegations of outbursts and misconduct. Feeling misunderstood, JD pushed back, recounting his experiences to offer his perspective. While careful not to reveal too much and risk triggering another intervention by child services, JD made it clear that his resistance to the move stemmed from a deep sense of entrapment. The therapist, recognizing his frustration, suggested JD consider living with his father.

The idea appealed to JD in part because his father's home offered structure and normalcy. Meals were eaten together as a family, arguments were mild and rare, and the environment lacked the volatility he had grown up with. For a short time, JD experienced the simplicity of family life: fishing, watching movies, and grilling steaks with his younger siblings. Yet even this stability felt alien. His father's strict religious beliefs and quiet demeanor created an undercurrent of uncertainty. JD avoided sharing personal interests, fearing judgment or rejection. The nagging sense of being on guard overshadowed the comforts of this new life.

Ultimately, JD decided to return to Middletown and Mamaw's house. Her unconditional love and fierce loyalty offered a sense of home he couldn't replicate elsewhere. When he called Lindsay for help, she responded without hesitation, driving over to bring him back. Reunited with Mamaw, JD felt the weight of his conflicts lift. Though he promised his mother he would live with her during the school year, his heart remained with Mamaw. The summer ended as it began— with JD seeking a balance between his need for independence and the family ties that anchored him.

A Front-Row Seat to Chaos

Living with Mom and Matt was chaos, though by JD's standards, it wasn't anything unusual. For Matt, however, it was a one-way ticket to disaster. As fights between Mom and Matt escalated, JD knew their relationship wouldn't last. Despite Matt's kindness, he became another victim of a family dynamic that couldn't sustain "nice guys."

Surprisingly, one day Mom announced she was getting married—not to Matt, but to Ken, her boss from the dialysis center. Within days, they moved into Ken's home in Miamisburg, making it JD's fourth home in just two years. The rapid transition left JD reeling, forced to adjust to a new environment and Ken's three children, who were just as baffled by the arrangement. Clashes were inevitable. When Ken's eldest son insulted Mom, JD's sense of Appalachian honor demanded a response. A near-violent confrontation followed, prompting Mom to take JD to Mamaw's for the night.

Amid this turmoil, JD reflected on systemic failures he saw in his struggling school district. He recognized that while debates over education policies like vouchers and reform were important, they overlooked a critical reality: many kids weren't just struggling in school but were battling chaotic home lives. As one teacher later told him, "They want us to be shepherds to these kids. But no one wants to talk about the fact that many of them are raised by wolves."

The instability took its toll. JD's sophomore year felt like a spiral. With a poor GPA, spotty attendance, and minimal effort in school, he flirted with failure. Experimenting with alcohol and marijuana—ironically sourced from Ken's greenhouse—added to his struggles. For the first time, he felt distant from Lindsay, who was thriving in her new life. Her stable marriage and devotion to her son contrasted sharply with JD's nomadic existence. While she seemed to escape their shared past, JD felt trapped, stuck in cycles of chaos and instability.

CHAPTER 8

The Breaking Point

JD Vance's life with his mother and her revolving door of relationships reached a pivotal moment during his sophomore year. He had been navigating the challenges of living with his new stepfather, Ken, and his children, but the cracks in this arrangement deepened quickly. The loneliness of being away from his sister, Lindsay, and Mamaw weighed heavily on him. Even the small comfort of maintaining his Middletown school routine couldn't mitigate the sense of alienation he felt in Ken's house.

The turning point came during a winter morning when JD's mother, Bev, burst into Mamaw's house, demanding a jar of clean urine to pass a drug test mandated by the nursing board. Her entitlement, devoid of guilt or shame, reflected a pattern of broken promises. She pleaded and cried, invoking the hope that had sustained their family through countless crises: the belief that if they just helped her this time, things would finally improve.

For JD, however, the demand was a step too far. He exploded, venting years of frustration. He called his mother a terrible parent and even criticized Mamaw for enabling her behavior. His anger was raw, but it cut deep. Mamaw's face drained of color, the sting of his words unmistakable. Despite his outburst, JD confided in Mamaw that he couldn't give his mother his urine because he had experimented with marijuana himself. Mamaw, as always, found a way to soften the situation. She reassured him that a few hits wouldn't show up on the test and invoked her enduring hope: "Maybe this time, she'll learn her lesson."

JD ultimately relented, giving in to Mamaw's unshakeable faith in the people she loved. But something inside him broke that morning. The humiliation of watching his mother struggle at a Chinese buffet, unable to control herself under the influence of prescription pills, had already frayed his patience. The urine episode solidified his realization that something had to change.

Mamaw reached her own breaking point. That evening, she declared that JD would live with her permanently. His mother, worn down by her own struggles, seemed indifferent to the decision, claiming she needed a break from motherhood. Not long after, her relationship with Ken ended, and JD moved in with Mamaw for good.

Life with Mamaw was far from easy, but it was stable. Her tough love came with sharp-tongued rebukes and unrelenting expectations: Get good grades, get a job, and help out around the house. Yet beneath her bark lay genuine care. She demanded effort but balanced it with humor and affection. JD often found himself laughing at her antics, like the time she tricked him into watching a murder mystery just so she could scare him at the perfect moment.

Though living with Mamaw tested JD's patience, it also provided the foundation he needed to rebuild his life. Her faith in him and her unyielding hope for the future gave him a stability he had never known.

Three Years That Saved Me

Living with Mamaw provided stability JD had never known, offering him a glimpse into her values, struggles, and resilience. Until those years, he hadn't fully grasped what made her tick. Her complex relationship with Jackson, Kentucky—once a refuge for JD—revealed itself as something far different to her. For Mamaw, Jackson was the source of childhood hunger, painful memories of teenage scandal, and the struggles of friends lost to the mines. While JD saw Jackson as a place of family and solace, Mamaw had escaped it and viewed returning as a duty rather than a joy.

Mamaw's quirks emerged in her old age. A lover of TV dramas like *The Sopranos*, she admired characters like Tony Soprano for their loyalty to family, even while criticizing their flaws—Tony's infidelity being a notable sore point. Her sense of humor and love for children also shone through. Whether teaching her young great-grandchildren not to mimic her colorful language or sharing a laugh over Kameron's innocent questions about profanity, Mamaw's affection for "those babies" was clear. It reflected her long-held dream of becoming a lawyer for abused and neglected children—a dream cut short by life's challenges.

Despite her love for family, Mamaw's physical health tested her resilience. A mistaken back surgery sent her to a nursing home for recovery, which she despised. She relied on JD and other family members to smuggle in Taco Bell, grumbling about the food and the indignities of institutional life. Even in such moments, her dark humor shone: she once demanded that JD promise to "end things" if she ever faced permanent confinement. Fortunately, a hip surgery resolved much of her pain, restoring some of her mobility.

JD's relationship with his mother remained strained. After one of her breakups, she spent time on Mamaw's couch, attempting to show affection through money rather than health or stability. JD didn't care about the money—he just wanted her to be well. Despite her flaws, he continued to love her while living under Mamaw's watchful eye.

At school, JD excelled, inspired partly by Mamaw's sacrifices. She ensured he had the best tools, like a state-of-the-art graphing calculator, and constantly reminded him of the importance of hard work. Her investment in his education made him realize the seriousness of school, even if it came with her usual sharp-tongued encouragement: "I didn't spend every penny I had on that little computer so you could fuck around all day."

Mamaw's unrelenting demands extended beyond academics. She insisted that JD get a job to learn the value of a dollar. Working as a cashier at Dillman's grocery store gave him insights into class divides and the struggles of the working poor. JD observed how harried customers purchased frozen and precooked food, contrasting with the deliberate, produce-filled carts of wealthier patrons. He also noticed how some gamed the welfare system—buying items with food stamps only to sell them for cash or ringing up separate transactions for essentials and luxuries like alcohol.

These lessons stirred mixed emotions in JD: frustration at the systemic inequalities and a sense of determination to rise above them. Dillman's revealed the quiet injustices of his world, where his people were seen as less trustworthy than those with Cadillacs and tabs. Yet, JD resolved that one day he'd have his own tab, symbolizing a future where he could stand on equal footing.

The three years living with Mamaw were transformative. Her tough love and unwavering support gave JD a foundation to thrive. Though she was difficult to live with—her sharp wit and demands often testing his patience—her influence was undeniable. Mamaw didn't just give him stability; she shaped his values and reminded him of his potential. By the end of those years, JD had begun to turn his life around, finding not only academic success but also the inner resilience that would carry him forward.

CHAPTER 9

Reading and Reflections

Living with Mamaw gave JD not just stability but also a lens to examine the struggles of his community. Mamaw's fiery spirit and sharp observations transformed their shared experiences at Dillman's grocery store into lessons about class, policy, and the fragile lives of those around them. JD's budding awareness of inequality, fueled by his readings, became a cornerstone of his intellectual and emotional journey.

At seventeen, JD worked at Dillman's and grew increasingly frustrated with what he saw. Every paycheck reminded him of the taxes deducted from his wages, money that seemed to benefit neighbors who abused welfare systems, buying T-bone steaks and other luxuries he couldn't afford. This anger mirrored sentiments shared by many in Appalachia, fueling a political shift from Democratic ideals to Republican skepticism about government programs.

Mamaw's own frustrations ran hot and cold. One day, she'd rail against Section 8 housing, calling it a system that brought "lazy" people into her neighborhood. The next, her bleeding-heart compassion emerged as she lamented the lack of jobs or drug treatment facilities. "We can afford aircraft carriers but not rehab centers," she'd grumble, blending social conservatism with progressive critiques. For JD, these contradictions initially seemed like inconsistencies, but over time, he came to see them as reflections of a deeply empathetic heart grappling with a broken system.

Their conversations often veered into the personal. When Section 8 housing arrived in their neighborhood, the families who moved in looked unsettlingly familiar. A Kentucky-born matriarch, abandoned by a string of men, raised children amidst late-night fights and drug use—circumstances all too close to JD's own family story. Mamaw's anger and heartbreak intertwined as she recognized herself in their struggles, even as she resented the dysfunction they brought.

This emotional complexity became a backdrop for JD's intellectual pursuits. Inspired by Mamaw's rants and his own questions, he began consuming books about social policy and poverty. William Julius Wilson's *The Truly Disadvantaged* resonated deeply. It described how factory closures left communities in economic and social freefall, isolating the poor and eroding support networks. Though Wilson wrote about inner-city Black communities, JD felt he could have been describing his own Appalachian roots. Similarly, Charles Murray's *Losing Ground* examined how government programs inadvertently enabled cycles of poverty, reinforcing JD's observations at Dillman's.

Still, these books didn't fully answer the questions that haunted him. Why did neighbors stay with abusive partners? Why did they spend money on drugs while neglecting their children? Why couldn't his mother break free from her own destructive patterns? The more he read, the more he realized that no single book or theory could explain the challenges facing his community. The issues were sociological, yes, but they were also deeply rooted in psychology, culture, faith, and the fragile fabric of human relationships.

JD found himself wrestling with the same heartbreak that consumed Mamaw. Behind every outburst or failing, there was pain. The neighbor's grim humor about her mother's violence wasn't just a joke— it was a shield, a way of enduring. JD recognized this because he had done the same, smiling through pain, laughing off struggles that cut to the bone. These moments weren't just stories of despair but evidence of a collective resilience, albeit one fraught with contradictions.

In quieter moments, JD would reflect on what all this meant for him. The problems weren't confined to his family or his neighborhood— they were systemic, entrenched, and deeply personal. Mamaw had believed she escaped the poverty of the hills, but its emotional weight had followed her, reshaping her later years into a mirror of her early struggles. This realization brought JD closer to her, deepening his understanding of her strength and flaws.

As JD's reading expanded, so did his perspective. He began to see his community not just as a collection of broken individuals but as part of a broader elegy—a story of cultural and economic dislocation. His growing awareness became a means of navigating his own path, one rooted in the recognition of both the pain and the resilience that defined his world.

Finding Happiness and Stability

During JD Vance's junior year of high school, his life began to take a turn for the better. The chaos of moving, the instability of family life, and the parade of strangers who entered and exited his world—all hallmarks of his childhood—gave way to something rare: peace. This transformation, centered around living permanently with Mamaw, became the foundation for his happiness and success.

For years, JD had lived a life defined by turmoil. The instability of constantly shifting between homes and caregivers left him with no sense of security. Each move uprooted him emotionally and physically, straining his relationships and his academic performance. By the end of ninth grade, he had cycled through a dizzying number of homes and parental figures. Drugs, domestic violence, and the interference of children's services compounded his anxiety. Amid this chaos, JD craved one thing: a stable home where he could grow without interruption.

Moving in with Mamaw permanently at the end of his sophomore year changed everything. For the first time, JD lived in the same house with the same person for years. By the end of his tenth, eleventh, and twelfth grades, he remained rooted in Mamaw's home—a stark contrast to the seven turbulent years before. This newfound stability allowed him to focus on school, build meaningful friendships, and start envisioning a future beyond Middletown.

Mamaw's home wasn't just a place of consistency; it was a sanctuary of encouragement and discipline. She held JD to high standards, demanding he excel academically and take responsibility for his life. She insisted on the importance of education, often reminding him that hard work was the path to success. When JD hesitated to do his homework, Mamaw's sharp tongue and unwavering belief in his potential spurred him into action. Her fierce support extended to small gestures that carried immense weight, like purchasing him a graphing calculator for an advanced math class, ensuring he had the tools to succeed.

But Mamaw's love was not just about discipline—it was deeply personal. She showed him what a stable, loving home could look like, even in its imperfections. She provided safety, humor, and moments of profound connection. One Sunday, as JD reluctantly left for his shift at Dillman's grocery store, he confessed to Mamaw that he wished he could stay home and spend the day with her and the babies she was babysitting. Instead of her usual sharp retort, she surprised him with empathy: "I wish you could stay home, too. But if you want the sort of work where you can spend the weekends with your family, you've got to go to college and make something of yourself."

That moment crystallized Mamaw's genius for JD She didn't just demand better from him; she showed him why it mattered. She painted a picture of the life he could have—a peaceful Sunday afternoon with loved ones—and made him believe it was within reach. Her unwavering love, combined with her tough-love approach, gave JD the tools and confidence to succeed.

The stability of Mamaw's home allowed JD to reflect on the chaos of his past and begin to chart a different course. He stopped experimenting with drugs, focused on his studies, and aced the SAT. He discovered a love for learning, inspired by teachers who recognized his potential. For the first time, he experienced the freedom that came from not living in constant fear of disruption. He no longer dreaded the school bell signaling the end of the day, unsure of what awaited him at home. Instead, he returned to a house filled with love, humor, and a grandmother who believed in him fiercely.

JD's happiness wasn't just a fleeting emotion; it became the bedrock of his transformation. The peace and security he found with Mamaw enabled him to thrive in ways he never imagined. It allowed him to dream beyond Middletown, to imagine a life where he could break free from the cycles of poverty and chaos that had defined his community.

The simplicity of Mamaw's home—free from drama, instability, and strangers—gave JD something priceless: hope. And from that hope emerged the opportunities that would shape his life for years to come.

CORPS

"We think of the Marine Corps as a military outfit, and of course it is, but for me, the U.S. Marine Corps was a four-year crash course in character education. It taught me how to make a bed, how to do laundry, how to wake up early, how to manage my finances. These are things my community didn't teach me."

CHAPTER 10

A Leap into the Unknown

During his senior year of high school, JD faced the weighty question of what to do with his future. College seemed the obvious choice—his friends were planning to attend, and he had worked hard to earn decent SAT scores. Yet, as the moment approached to commit to Ohio State, doubts crept in. College required independence and grit—qualities JD wasn't sure he possessed. "It's the only damned thing worth spending money on right now," Mamaw said as they pored over financial aid forms together. But the cost and uncertainty loomed large, making the decision feel overwhelming.

A suggestion from his cousin Rachael, a Marine Corps veteran, changed everything. "They'll whip your ass into shape," she told him, with the authority of someone who had been through it herself. JD respected Rachael deeply, and her words planted a seed of possibility. The idea of the Marines, terrifying and unthinkable just weeks earlier, began to feel like a real option. The timing seemed perfect: the 9/11 attacks had stirred a sense of patriotism, and the Iraq War was ramping up. JD thought, like many young men from his background, that he might find meaning and purpose by serving his country.

Still, he hesitated. The Marines promised discipline, structure, and the kind of transformation he knew he needed, but they also promised hardship. "They'll chew you up and spit you out," Mamaw said bluntly when he broached the idea. Her words were a mix of worry and frustration. She feared losing him, not just to the dangers of war but to the distance the military would inevitably create. "You're too stupid for the Marines," she teased one moment, only to counter it the next with, "You're too smart for the Marines."

Mamaw wasn't the only one with reservations. His family initially scoffed at the idea, doubting that the pudgy, long-haired kid who avoided running in gym class could make it through Marine boot camp. But JD's mind was set. "The GI Bill will keep me out of debt," he explained, hoping to soften their resistance. More importantly, he saw the Marines as a way to become the disciplined, capable adult he wanted to be.

One Saturday in March, JD walked into a recruiter's office to learn more. The recruiter didn't sugarcoat the experience. "You'll make very little money, and you might go to war," he said, "but they'll teach you about leadership, and they'll turn you into a disciplined young man." Those words stuck with JD The thought of rising every morning at five A.M. and running miles was daunting, but the promise of transformation outweighed his fears. He knew if he didn't act quickly, he'd talk himself out of it. Two weeks later, as the Iraq crisis escalated into war, JD signed the papers and committed to four years with the Marine Corps.

The decision caused a stir at home. Over time, most of his family came around, even expressing a bit of pride. Mamaw, however, never fully accepted it. "Don't you want to be around for Lindsay's kids?" she asked, desperate to dissuade him. She worried endlessly about his safety, his ability to endure the rigorous training, and the possibility that he wouldn't come back. When JD's recruiter visited the house to reassure her, Mamaw met him in the yard. "Set one foot on my fucking porch, and I'll blow it off," she warned. The recruiter stayed firmly on the grass.

Despite her protests, JD knew Mamaw was proud in her way. But her resistance highlighted his own fears. It wasn't combat or boot camp that terrified him most—it was the thought of losing her. As his family drove him to the bus that would take him to boot camp, JD couldn't shake the feeling that Mamaw wouldn't live to see him return. Her declining health and the toll of her life's struggles loomed large. Middletown with Mamaw was home, and the idea of a life without her felt unimaginable. Signing up for the Marines was a leap into adulthood, but it also marked the beginning of a goodbye he wasn't ready to face.

The night before he left, JD and Mamaw sat in the living room, neither willing to say what they both felt. "You're going to do great things, kid," she said finally, her voice softer than usual. JD nodded, but inside, he was afraid. Afraid of failing, of losing the only person who had ever been his constant, and of the unknown world that awaited him. Yet, deep down, he knew this decision would define his life.

Lessons Beyond the Yellow Footprints

Marine Corps boot camp began with a crash course in discipline the moment JD arrived at Parris Island. As he stepped off the bus, an angry drill instructor barked orders, herding the recruits onto the famed yellow footprints. From there, the night descended into controlled chaos: medical evaluations, uniform fittings, haircuts, and a brief, scripted phone call. "I have arrived safely at Parris Island. I will send my address soon. Goodbye," JD recited when he called Mamaw. Her response, "Wait, you little shithead. Are you okay?" was met with a hurried "Sorry, Mamaw, can't talk. I'll write as soon as I can," earning him a sarcastic remark from the drill instructor for the unsanctioned banter. That was day one.

Communication during boot camp was limited to letters, and JD's family seized the opportunity to flood him with words of encouragement. Mamaw wrote daily, sometimes multiple times. Her letters ranged from reflections on life to disjointed streams of consciousness, but their constant theme was reassurance: "You're smart, and I know you won't give up," she reminded him over and over. Those letters were a lifeline. Amid grueling physical challenges and unrelenting discipline, JD drew strength from knowing his family was behind him.

Letters from Mom and Lindsay brought snippets of home life. Mom wrote about babysitting her grandchildren, her humor shining through: "Kam played with a slug, squished it, and thought he killed it. I threw it away and told him he didn't because he got upset." In the same breath, she mentioned a boyfriend and casually noted, "Mandy's husband Terry was arrested on a probation violation. So they're all doing okay." Lindsay, ever the doting mother, filled her letters with updates about her children, sharing milestones like potty training and soccer matches.

Boot camp was a melting pot of backgrounds, and JD found camaraderie with those who shared his Appalachian roots. In one letter home, he described a fellow recruit from Leslie County, Kentucky, who didn't know what a Catholic was. Mamaw's reply was pure Bonnie "Down in that part of Kentucky, everybody's a snake handler."

Despite her humor, Mamaw's vulnerability surfaced while JD was away. She called Lindsay and others to help decipher his letters, and her own writing revealed her longing: "I keep thinking you'll come down the stairs so I can holler at you. It's just a feeling you aren't really gone." Yet her fierce loyalty remained intact. After JD faced a grueling punishment from a drill instructor, Mamaw unleashed her wrath in a letter: "Them dick-face bastards piss me off. I hate all of them." The next day, she doubled down: "Screaming is part of their game, but you'll come out ahead because you're smart and they know it."

Boot camp meals were a study in efficiency. Recruits had just minutes to eat without moving their heads or looking at their plates. Dessert was optional, but when JD grabbed a piece of cake on the first day, a drill instructor snarled, "You really need that cake, don't you, fat-ass?" before swatting it out of his hands. JD never reached for dessert again.

That moment, like many others in boot camp, held deeper significance. In the past, an insult like that might have crushed his confidence. Instead, JD found himself adapting and persevering. The constant challenges of boot camp—physical, emotional, and mental—forced him to confront the self-doubt that had shadowed him since childhood. Each obstacle he overcame, no matter how small, chipped away at his insecurities.

By the end of those thirteen weeks, JD began to see himself differently. The Marine Corps didn't just demand discipline; it revealed reserves of strength he hadn't known he possessed. What had started as an overwhelming challenge became a transformative experience, one that left him not only physically stronger but also more assured in his ability to face the world.

The Marine Corps taught him something he'd never fully grasped before: he was capable of far more than he had ever imagined.

CHAPTER 11

The Marine Corps and Becoming a Protector

Marine Corps boot camp is designed to break recruits down to their core and rebuild them with a new identity. Individuality dissolves as recruits are stripped of their names, forbidden to say "I," and required to refer to themselves only as "this recruit." Every detail of life was scrutinized, down to tattoos that drew relentless ridicule. By the time boot camp ended, only sixty-nine out of the original eighty-three recruits in JD Vance's platoon remained. Those who dropped out, mostly for medical reasons, became constant reminders of how grueling the challenge was and how valuable the title of "marine" would be.

For JD, boot camp didn't just train his body; it reshaped his mind. Each day brought small victories: keeping pace on a grueling run, conquering the seemingly impossible rope climb, or withstanding the relentless yelling of drill instructors. These moments taught him to challenge the helplessness that had defined much of his youth. "Every time I thought I couldn't do something and then did it," JD reflected, "I came a little closer to believing in myself."

Graduation day was a pinnacle moment. An entourage of eighteen hillbillies—including Mamaw, frail but determined in her wheelchair—traveled to Parris Island to celebrate his achievement. JD beamed as he showed his family around the base, filled with pride. When he returned to Middletown on leave, he noticed a palpable shift in how people treated him. At the barbershop, where he'd been going for years, the barber greeted him with respect, trading jokes and refusing payment for the haircut. It was the first time JD had felt like an equal in the adult world.

Back in Middletown, his physical transformation also drew attention. Having shed forty-five pounds, he was nearly unrecognizable to old friends. Even his diet had changed. Mamaw's kitchen, once a haven of fried delights and cobblers, now seemed an assault on his newfound health consciousness. "Is there added sugar?" he'd ask about blackberry cobbler. "How much salt is in this meat?" It wasn't just food—JD realized that the Marine Corps had reshaped his perspective on everything, including the town he'd once called home.

Soon, JD left for his permanent Marine Corps assignment, but he kept close ties to his family. Frequent phone calls and leave trips every few months allowed him to stay connected. Despite his fears before boot camp, life at home carried on without major upheavals. Mamaw's health improved slightly, and she even gained weight. Lindsay and Aunt Wee's families thrived. Even Mom moved in with Mamaw temporarily, providing moments of closeness and stability that had long eluded them.

In January 2005, JD's unit received orders to deploy to Iraq. The announcement filled him with a mix of pride and anxiety. When he called Mamaw to share the news, the phone went silent. After a long pause, she muttered, "I hope the war ends before you have to go." Though they spoke frequently in the months leading up to his deployment, the topic of Iraq never came up again. JD knew she was avoiding it, and he respected her wishes.

Mamaw's health struggles persisted. When AK Steel raised her health insurance premiums by $300 a month, she confided in JD that she couldn't afford the increase. Without hesitation, he offered to cover the costs. It was a poignant moment: Mamaw, who had always refused his financial help, accepted this time. "That's how I knew she was desperate," JD later admitted.

Though he earned modestly as a marine, JD supplemented his income through online poker, earning an extra $400 a month. Poker, a pastime he'd learned from Papaw and his great-uncles, now became a way to provide for his family. When Mamaw expressed concern about his "gambling," JD reassured her. "It's online, Mamaw. I'm not sitting in a smoky trailer with card sharks." She relented but warned, "Just don't start drinking and chasing women. That's what always happens to dipshits who gamble."

Paying for Mamaw's insurance marked a shift in their dynamic. Mamaw had always been JD's protector, but now he was stepping into that role. It wasn't just about the money. On trips home, JD delighted in treating his family—buying lunch for Mom, ice cream for the kids, and small gifts for Lindsay. One memorable trip to Hocking Hills with Mamaw, Lindsay, and her children left JD brimming with pride as he covered gas, dinner, and other expenses. "For the first time," he recalled, "I felt like a real grown-up, a man who could take care of his family."

Reflecting on his journey, JD likened his life to the movie *Terminator*

2, a favorite he often watched with Mamaw. To him, Mamaw was his protector, a fierce guardian who could fight off any danger. But paying for her health insurance flipped the script. "For the first time in my life, I felt like I was the protector," JD said. "I wasn't just surviving; I was providing."

This newfound sense of empowerment was transformative. For years, JD had oscillated between fear and fleeting moments of stability, always dependent on others to shield him from chaos. But now, for the first time, he understood the satisfaction of creating stability for those he loved. "Mamaw could preach about responsibility and hard work all she wanted," JD reflected, "but no speech could have taught me how it feels to go from seeking shelter to providing it."

The Marine Corps had given him more than discipline and strength; it had shown him that he could shoulder responsibility and thrive. It was a lesson he carried with him, one that reshaped not just his life but his entire identity. For JD, becoming a protector wasn't just about fulfilling Mamaw's dreams—it was about fulfilling his own.

CHAPTER 12

A Transformative Event

Mamaw's seventy-second birthday was just around the corner in April 2005. A few days before, JD stood in the waiting room of a Walmart Supercenter, waiting for his car's oil change. He called Mamaw on the cell phone he now paid for himself. She was babysitting Lindsay's kids that day and recounted one of Meghan's mischievous antics. "Meghan is so damned cute," she said, laughing. "I told her to shit in the pot, and for three hours she just kept saying, 'shit in the pot, shit in the pot.' I told her to stop, or I'd get in trouble, but she wouldn't." JD laughed along with her, told her he loved her, and reminded her that her $300 check was on the way. "JD, thank you for helping me," she replied warmly. "I'm very proud of you, and I love you." Those were her last words to him.

Two days later, JD was woken by a call from Lindsay. Mamaw's lung had collapsed, she explained, and she was in a coma. The situation was dire, and Lindsay urged him to come home quickly. JD packed his dress blue Marine uniform, unsure if he'd need it for a funeral, and began the thirteen-hour drive to Middletown. On the way, a West Virginia police officer pulled him over for speeding. Hearing his explanation, the officer handed him a warning ticket and said, "The road's clear of speed traps for the next seventy miles. Go as fast as you need." JD drove at top speed and reached the hospital in under eleven hours.

At Middletown Regional Hospital, the family was gathered around Mamaw's bed. She was unresponsive, and while her lung had been reinflated, the infection that caused the collapse wasn't improving. The doctor explained that her chances of recovery were slim without a ventilator and feeding tube. After days of waiting and worsening signs, the family made the agonizing decision: if her condition didn't improve within a day, they would remove life support. Legally, the decision rested with Aunt Wee, who tearfully asked JD if she was making a mistake. He reassured her, though doubt lingered for everyone.

When the ventilator was removed, the doctor predicted Mamaw would pass within fifteen minutes, maybe an hour at most. But true to her indomitable spirit, she lasted three hours. The family surrounded her, taking turns whispering goodbyes. As her heart rate slowed, JD opened a Gideon's Bible to a random passage: "For now we see through a glass, darkly; but then face to face: now I know in part; but then shall I know even as also I am known." Moments later, Mamaw was gone.

JD didn't cry. Days passed, and still, he held his emotions in check. Lindsay and Aunt Wee grew concerned. "You're too stoic, JD," they told him. "You need to let it out." But JD felt the weight of holding the family together. The aftermath of Mamaw's death brought new pressures. Debts had to be settled, the estate managed, and property divided. For the first time, Uncle Jimmy discovered the extent of Mom's financial strain on Mamaw—the rehab costs, unpaid loans, and constant bailouts. It severed his relationship with Mom; he hasn't spoken to her since.

Mamaw's generosity left the estate with little. Papaw's decades of savings amounted only to their house. Fortunately, this was 2005, during the height of the real estate bubble. Had she died three years later, the estate would have been bankrupt. Her will divided assets equally among her three children, except for Mom's share, which was split between JD and Lindsay. This sparked inevitable drama with Mom, who descended into familiar patterns of emotional turmoil.

Mamaw's funeral followed her wishes: a visitation in Middletown, a service in Jackson, Kentucky, and burial at the family cemetery in Keck. The convoy to Keck, winding through narrow mountain roads, was steeped in memories. Each turn recalled stories of family, laughter, and adventure. But instead of sharing these memories, the car was filled with Mom's bitter outbursts. "You two are too sad," she snapped at Lindsay and JD "She was my mom, not yours!"

For JD, this was the breaking point. Years of making excuses for Mom, enduring her addiction, and trying to help her had taken a toll. Lindsay spoke before JD could unleash his anger. "No, Mom," she said firmly. "She was our mom, too." Her words hung in the air, silencing any further argument.

The day after the funeral, JD returned to North Carolina to rejoin his Marine Corps unit. Driving through the Virginia mountains, he hit a wet patch of road on a sharp turn. The car spun out of control, hurtling toward the guardrail. For a fleeting moment, he thought this was the end—that he'd join Mamaw sooner than expected. But as if by a miracle, the car stopped just short of the edge. Whether by luck or something more, JD felt Mamaw's presence, steadying him one last time.

Shaken, he pulled to the side of the road and finally let the tears flow. He called Lindsay and Aunt Wee before continuing his journey to the base.

From the Marines to a New Beginning

JD's final two years in the Marine Corps were a whirlwind of routine, discipline, and learning experiences, punctuated by a few memorable moments that defined the man he was becoming. It was a period of transformation, pushing him to test limits he hadn't known he could reach and reshaping his perception of himself and the world.

One such moment took place in Iraq, where JD had been deployed as a public affairs marine. His job was to document stories about his fellow marines and their work, occasionally escorting members of the civilian press. Early in the deployment, he joined a civil affairs unit on a mission to connect with local Iraqi communities. These missions were considered risky, as small groups of marines ventured into unsecured territories to interact with locals.

On this particular day, senior marines met with school officials while the rest of the team distributed supplies and played with the children. JD handed out candy and school supplies, blending into the vibrant, chaotic energy of the schoolyard. Among the children, one boy stood out. Shy and hesitant, he approached JD and held out his hand. JD placed a small eraser in his palm, and the boy's face lit up with uncontainable joy before he ran off to show his family, holding the eraser aloft like a trophy.

That moment stayed with JD long after. It didn't erase the anger and resentment he'd carried for years—anger at his chaotic childhood, at a life of constant struggle, at feeling deprived of what others had. But it sparked a profound realization: JD recognized how much he had to be grateful for. He had been born in a country of opportunity, raised by two flawed but deeply loving grandparents, and now belonged to a family that, despite its dysfunction, had always cared for him. Seeing joy in something as small as an eraser made JD want to strive for that same gratitude in his own life. He wasn't there yet, but he resolved to try.

The Marine Corps shaped JD in countless ways, instilling habits and lessons that went far beyond combat training. From the start, the Marines assumed ignorance in their recruits and filled the gaps with a relentless focus on life skills. JD learned to balance a checkbook, compare interest rates, and prioritize saving. When he showed up with a mediocre loan for a car, a fellow marine dragged him to a credit union and showed him how to secure a better rate. The Marines didn't just train soldiers; they shaped responsible adults.

Physical transformation came alongside mental growth. The boy who once dreaded gym class and struggled to run a mile became a man who could climb a thirty-foot rope using only one arm. He shaved minutes off his running times, stood taller, and carried himself with a newfound confidence. More importantly, he began to see himself as a leader. JD learned that effective leadership wasn't about barking orders but about earning respect and showing respect in return. He worked alongside people from every imaginable background and watched as shared goals and mutual respect transformed disparate individuals into a cohesive family.

One of his most challenging assignments came during his last nine months of service. Due to a lack of available officers, JD was thrust into the role of media relations officer for Cherry Point, one of the largest Marine Corps bases on the East Coast. It was a daunting task—live TV interviews, liaising with senior officers, and managing high-stakes press coverage for events like the base's massive air show. JD made mistakes, such as allowing photographers too close to a classified aircraft, but his superiors guided him through those errors. With time, he improved and earned a commendation medal for his work during the air show. The experience proved that he could handle responsibilities far beyond what he once thought possible.

These lessons weren't just about practical skills; they reshaped how JD viewed himself and his potential. Growing up in Middletown, he had internalized the belief that people like him were inherently limited. The Marine Corps shattered that notion. Through relentless demands and unwavering expectations, the Corps replaced feelings of helplessness with an understanding that effort and determination could overcome almost any obstacle.

When his time in the Marines ended, JD packed his discharge papers and hopped into his first major purchase: a used Honda Civic. He drove from Cherry Point, North Carolina, back to Middletown, Ohio, reflecting on everything he had experienced. In four years, he had seen the desperation of war-torn Iraq and the aftermath of natural disasters in Haiti. He had lost Mamaw and gone to war shortly afterward. He had made lifelong friends and proven to himself that he was capable of more than he had ever imagined.

Most importantly, the Marines had prepared him for the next chapter of his life. He was no longer the teenager who couldn't fill out a financial aid form or keep a steady job. Now, he knew exactly what he wanted and how to achieve it. In three weeks, he would begin classes at Ohio State University, ready to embrace a future that once felt out of reach.

COLLEGE

'I have never felt out of place in my entire life.
But I did at Yale.'

CHAPTER 13

A New Chapter: Thriving at Ohio State

JD arrived at Ohio State in September 2007, thrilled to begin a new chapter. Everything about that day felt monumental—the Chipotle lunch with Lindsay (her first time trying it), the sunny walk to his soon-to-be campus home, and the simplicity of his four-day class schedule with no early mornings. After years of grueling Marine Corps wake-ups, this felt like a dream.

Ohio State's proximity to Middletown—just a hundred miles away—meant JD could visit home easily. Unlike Havelock, the unremarkable North Carolina town near his Marine base, Columbus was alive with energy. The city was expanding, with new businesses, revitalized neighborhoods, and a vibrant cultural scene. A friend's job at a local radio station gave JD access to the best events, from festivals to fireworks, making Columbus feel like an exciting urban paradise.

In many ways, college felt familiar. JD's six roommates were all from southwest Ohio, most from Middletown High, creating a sense of home away from home. Yet he noticed a stark trend: many small-town friends who came to Ohio State never returned, part of the "brain drain" where opportunity lured people away from struggling hometowns. Years later, he'd realize that his groomsmen, all from small Ohio towns, had done exactly the same.

Unlike his high school years, JD now thrived academically. The Marines had given him discipline and confidence. He juggled a packed schedule of classes, library study sessions, and late nights with friends, waking early to run without hesitation. The independence that once scared him now felt natural. He paid his bills, earned straight As, and planned for law school with clarity, knowing his success at Ohio State was key to his future. For the first time, JD felt entirely in control of his destiny.

Balancing Act

JD despised debt and the constraints it brought. Despite the GI Bill covering much of his tuition and Ohio State's reasonable in-state fees, he still faced a $20,000 gap. To bridge it, he took a job at the Ohio Statehouse, working for Senator Bob Schuler, a kind man with politics

JD admired. Handling constituent calls and observing legislative debates, JD gained a new respect for the political process. "Mamaw thought all politicians were crooks," he reflected, "but I learned that wasn't true, at least not at the Ohio Statehouse."

Still, the bills mounted, and desperate for more income, JD sought a second job. After an unsuccessful interview at a nonprofit, he adjusted his approach, bought more professional attire, and landed a consulting position with a group supporting abused and neglected children. With two jobs and a full class schedule, JD thrived on the intensity. When a professor urged him to focus more on academics, JD politely dismissed the advice. "I liked staying up late for assignments, running on little sleep, and proving I could handle it," he said.

However, this relentless pace took a toll. Ignoring the symptoms of what he thought was a cold, JD worked and studied until his body forced him to stop. When his urine turned brown and his temperature hit 103, he finally sought help. Diagnosed with mono and a staph infection, JD ended up in the hospital. Mom, hearing of his condition, drove to Columbus, supervising his care with the precision of a nurse. For two days, she ensured he received proper treatment, asking sharp questions and ensuring he was hydrated and monitored.

Mom's nurturing during his illness contrasted with the emotional strain of staying at her home during recovery. Splitting time between Mom's and Aunt Wee's houses, JD felt torn. While Mom's care was flawless during his illness, memories of past instability haunted him. Her fifth husband, a kind yet distant figure, reminded him of the many father figures who had come and gone. He couldn't reconcile these contradictions, saying, "I couldn't feel at home with her, no matter how much she tried."

The growing closeness between JD and Aunt Wee further strained his relationship with Mom. "I'm your mother, not her," she'd often remind him. JD wondered if his distance hurt her recovery, but self-preservation outweighed guilt. "I wasn't that person anymore," he admitted. "I couldn't be the one to hold her together."

Back in Columbus, JD resumed classes, lighter by twenty pounds but determined. With mounting medical bills, he added a third job as an SAT tutor, earning a much-needed $18 an hour. Though he enjoyed his work at the Ohio Senate, it paid the least, so he reluctantly let it go. "I needed financial freedom," he reasoned. "The rewarding work would come later."

And through it all, JD's resolve hardened.

CHAPTER 14

A Path to Optimism Amid Decline

JD's final years before law school revealed the intertwining themes of resilience, identity, and the weight of cultural pessimism in his community. While studying at Ohio State and navigating financial challenges, he found himself grappling with his own beliefs and the shifting values of his hometown.

One experience at the Ohio Senate encapsulated his evolving perspective. As lawmakers debated a bill to restrict payday lending, JD saw a disconnect between their intentions and the realities of the working poor. For him, payday loans were sometimes a lifeline, like when he used one to cover a rent check and avoid costly late fees. "Powerful people sometimes help people like me without understanding people like me," he realized. This moment deepened his appreciation for nuanced policymaking and its real-life impact.

His second year at Ohio State mirrored the first—heavily focused on academics and work. But at 24, JD felt a growing separation from younger classmates, heightened by his Marine Corps experience. A class discussion on the Iraq war brought this divide into sharp relief. Listening to a peer's baseless claim that soldiers were mindless and violent, JD contrasted it with his memories of Iraqi cultural training, his friends' sacrifices, and the humanity he witnessed among Iraqi civilians. That moment ignited a desire to finish school quickly. Overloading on courses and summer classes, he completed his degree in under two years, graduating summa cum laude.

Returning to Middletown after graduation, JD found solace living with his Aunt Wee, who had become the family's anchor after Mamaw's passing. Those months were among the happiest of his life. "This is your home now," Aunt Wee told him, offering stability and a sense of belonging. Surrounded by family, he felt the joy of normalcy—working odd jobs, helping his young cousins with homework, and participating in community events like fish fries at the local Catholic church.

Yet, the optimism he felt about his own life starkly contrasted with the growing despair in Middletown. The Great Recession had deepened the community's struggles, compounding years of economic decline. JD noticed not just financial hardship but also a spiritual and cultural detachment. Heroes and unifying symbols of pride seemed absent. Politicians, whether Barack Obama or George W. Bush, failed to inspire many residents. The military, long a source of admiration, lacked a modern figurehead like Patton or MacArthur. Even the space program, once a beacon of American achievement, had faded into history.

For JD, this cultural detachment struck at the heart of his identity. Raised by Mamaw and Papaw, he learned to love his country with unwavering faith. Their stories of World War II sacrifices—rationing, letters from the Pacific, and the pride of victory—shaped his worldview. "Mamaw had two gods: Jesus Christ and the United States of America," he reflected. Patriotism wasn't just a sentiment; it was a guiding force that gave meaning to his childhood and hope for a better future.

JD saw his patriotism as a source of strength, even if it felt outdated to others. "I choke up when I hear 'Proud to Be an American,'" he admitted, vowing from a young age to honor every veteran he met. This unwavering belief in America's greatness fueled his determination to succeed. "When times were tough, I knew better days were ahead because I lived in a country that allowed me to make the good choices others hadn't."

But for many in Middletown, that belief in America had eroded. The community's pride in its country—once akin to a shared religion—seemed to vanish under the weight of economic hardship and cultural cynicism. For JD, this loss symbolized a deeper fracture in the ties that once bound his hometown together.

As he prepared for law school, JD carried with him the lessons of resilience and hope instilled by Mamaw and Papaw. Despite the challenges of his upbringing and the despair surrounding him, he held fast to the idea that better days were possible—and that his journey was a testament to the enduring promise of the American Dream.

The Distrust and Alienation of Working-Class Whites

In many parts of America, a deep sense of alienation fueled distrust and anger toward institutions and figures of authority. For countless working-class whites, Barack Obama embodied this divide. Conservative voters frequently espoused unfounded beliefs about him: that he was foreign-born, a Muslim, or tied to Islamic extremists. These sentiments, while often appearing rooted in racism, stemmed more profoundly from cultural disconnects. Obama, as a product of

Ivy League education and urban sophistication, represented a world far removed from the daily lives of struggling communities. His polished demeanor, academic credentials, and perceived confidence only heightened insecurities about declining blue-collar prospects.

This mistrust extended beyond Obama to the media itself. Despite major news organizations repeatedly debunking conspiracy theories about his religion or birthplace, a significant portion of working-class whites rejected these truths. Only a fraction of voters considered the press trustworthy, and this skepticism left many vulnerable to online misinformation. Conspiracy theories proliferated in this environment: claims of government involvement in the 9/11 attacks, fears of microchip implantation through Obamacare, and assertions that the Newtown shooting had been staged to push gun control. These narratives, though outrageous, resonated in communities struggling with economic and cultural erosion. The distrust reflected a broader crisis—a community grappling with its place in a rapidly changing America.

Cultural Decline and Lost Optimism in the White Working Class

In struggling communities like Middletown, skepticism toward institutions ran deep. A significant portion of residents clung to conspiracy theories about Barack Obama's origins or policies, reflecting a broader mistrust of government, media, and universities. This cynicism wasn't a healthy skepticism—it was an entrenched belief that society had been rigged against them, sapping ambition and participation in civic life.

Social psychologists often linked collective beliefs to performance: groups who trusted the system tended to work harder and achieve more. But among working-class whites, pessimism dominated. The Pew Economic Mobility Project found that only 44 percent of working-class whites believed their children would fare better economically—a level of optimism lower than that of any other demographic group. Many in these communities blamed external forces, such as the government, for personal failures. This tendency fostered a culture of detachment and inertia, where ambition faltered, and civic engagement dwindled.

In contrast, the rare success stories within these communities often stemmed from high expectations and self-accountability. For JD, breaking away from this defeatist mindset required embracing optimism and pursuing education. However, his path to success also came with a cost—it felt like a cultural alienation. As he strove to overcome the limitations of his upbringing, JD often found himself caught between the values instilled in his childhood and the demands of a world that seemed worlds apart from the community he once called home.

CHAPTER 15

From Middletown to Yale

When JD first applied to law schools, Yale, Harvard, and Stanford seemed unattainable. His focus was practical: any law school would do, as he assumed all lawyers secured good jobs. This belief wavered when his best friend Darrell encountered a law school graduate bussing tables in D.C.—a stark reality check about the unpredictable job market. On his next round of applications, JD decided to aim higher, though self-doubt lingered.

Stanford's application required a form signed by the college dean—a seemingly trivial task, but one that triggered deep-seated mistrust in JD He couldn't bring himself to ask an unfamiliar authority figure to vouch for him, so he abandoned Stanford entirely. Yale, however, required no such hurdle, and applying was easy. Though he doubted his chances, he submitted his application anyway, treating it as a shot in the dark.

One spring day in 2010, an unfamiliar number from a 203 area code appeared on JD's phone. Answering, he heard the Yale Law admissions director announce his acceptance. Overwhelmed with joy, JD leaped around during the short call, his excitement so palpable that when he phoned Aunt Wee afterward, she feared he'd been in an accident. Yale wasn't just a dream come true—it was an opportunity to attend one of the best schools in the world with a financial aid package that made it cheaper than many state schools.

JD reflected on the irony: many low-income students avoid applying to elite schools, assuming they can't afford them. Yet, Yale's need-based aid made it his most affordable option. This realization underscored a systemic issue—bright students from disadvantaged backgrounds often miss out on opportunities because they lack accurate information about costs.

Leaving Middletown Behind

Preparing to leave for Yale felt different from previous moves. Joining the Marines or attending Ohio State were temporary departures, but this time, JD knew he wasn't coming back. Middletown no longer felt like home. He spent the summer working at a tile warehouse to save money for the transition and braced himself for a new chapter in New Haven.

Arriving at Yale was surreal. The campus felt like "nerd Hollywood," with prominent figures like Tony Blair and George Pataki casually appearing in hallways. Events that would draw massive crowds elsewhere were intimate gatherings at Yale. The grandeur of the neo-Gothic architecture and the school's storied history added to the sense of awe.

Yale's law school offered a surprisingly low-pressure start. The first semester was credit/no credit, allowing students to explore their interests without stressing about grades. JD joined a constitutional law seminar where his classmates became like family. Their diverse backgrounds—ranging from a neuroscientist to a civil rights advocate—created a tight-knit group affectionately dubbed the "island of misfit toys."

Despite his initial fears, JD found the academic workload manageable. He expected Yale's students to be intimidating geniuses, but most were simply smart, driven individuals. However, not everything came easily. A professor's harsh critique of his writing challenged him to improve. Determined to prove himself, JD worked hard to change the professor's opinion, eventually earning praise for his progress. This victory reaffirmed his ability to succeed in an elite environment.

For all his triumphs, Yale also planted seeds of doubt. The school's social rituals—cocktail receptions and networking events—felt alien. Though outwardly he fit the mold of an Ivy League student, JD couldn't shake the feeling that he was out of place. Back home, Ivy League graduates were non-existent, and his journey to Yale was unprecedented in his family.

The weight of Yale's legacy was palpable. The institution had educated Supreme Court justices, presidents, and secretaries of state. Its influence in shaping American leadership was undeniable, yet it was far removed from the world JD had grown up in. At times, the contrast felt jarring, and he wrestled with imposter syndrome. Could someone from Middletown truly belong in the halls of such power and privilege?

Despite these doubts, JD thrived. By the end of his first year, he had formed strong relationships with professors, earned solid grades, and secured a prestigious summer position with the chief counsel for a U.S. senator. His experiences at Yale expanded his horizons, reshaped his aspirations, and reinforced the value of hard work.

Yet, the journey also highlighted systemic barriers. JD's story illustrated how misinformation and self-doubt prevent many talented individuals from pursuing opportunities they're qualified for. His path to Yale wasn't just a personal achievement; it was a testament to the transformative power of ambition, perseverance, and access to accurate information.

As the first year ended, JD felt a mix of triumph and humility. Yale had challenged him, but it also showed him that his potential was far greater than he'd imagined.

Navigating Yale Law

At Yale Law School, JD found himself surrounded by a starkly different world, one defined by privilege and wealth. A survey revealed that over 95 percent of his classmates came from upper-middle-class or wealthy backgrounds. This contrasted sharply with his own experience growing up in Middletown, Ohio. Though diversity was celebrated at Yale, it was a diversity that often excluded socio-economic variance. Regardless of race or religion, most students came from intact families and had never faced financial hardship.

The class divide struck JD early. After a night of drinking with classmates, the group left a mess at a local chicken joint. Feeling it wrong to leave the cleanup to underpaid staff, JD stayed behind to tidy up. Only one classmate, Jamil, who also came from a less privileged background, helped him. Reflecting on the moment, JD realized they were likely the only two in the group who had ever cleaned up someone else's mess for a living.

In Middletown, JD had never felt out of place. Most families there shared a similar working-class background, and even the relatively wealthy among them weren't so far removed from his own experience. Yale, however, felt like a foreign land. Classmates referred to families earning six-figure incomes as "middle-class" and discussed future salaries of $160,000 as barely adequate. JD couldn't help but compare this to the realities of his upbringing, where such amounts were unimaginable.

CHAPTER 16

Intrigue and Alienation

At Yale, JD became a subject of curiosity. His background, which seemed unremarkable to him, intrigued professors and peers alike. Few of his classmates had encountered someone from a place like Middletown, and even fewer had interacted with a Marine Corps veteran. While this made JD unique, it also reinforced his sense of being an outsider.

At first, JD embraced this distinction. Being "the big Marine with a Southern twang" gave him an identity at Yale. Yet as acquaintances turned into friends, he began grappling with the lies he told to mask his past. "My mom is a nurse," he'd say, though she no longer worked in that profession. He rarely mentioned his father or the tumultuous upbringing that had shaped him. Over time, JD realized he didn't want to hide his story. His grandparents' influence had been profound, and he felt a need to honor their role in his life.

The decision to open up about his past marked a turning point. JD stopped feeling ashamed of his family's struggles. Instead, he saw his success as a testament to their support and resilience. However, this newfound pride didn't eliminate the inner conflict he felt about his place at Yale.

One encounter at a gas station during a visit home illustrated JD's internal struggle. Spotting a woman in a Yale T-shirt, he struck up a conversation and asked if she had attended the school. "No," she replied, "but my nephew does. Do you?" Confronted with her question, JD hesitated. Despite her nephew's connection to Yale, he imagined her as someone who might mock people like him at fancy dinners. In an impulsive act of defiance, he lied: "No, I don't go to Yale. But my girlfriend does." Then he quickly left.

This incident reflected a deeper tension in JD's life. On one hand, he was a proud Yale Law student, thriving in an elite institution. On the other, he couldn't shake the fear of betraying his roots. Success felt like a bridge to a world that didn't entirely accept him, and he struggled to reconcile the two identities.

JD's journey at Yale underscored the challenges of rapid upward mobility. The sense of alienation he experienced was both external—rooted in the stark differences between his upbringing and those of his classmates—and internal, as he wrestled with feelings of guilt and loyalty to his origins. His story highlighted the barriers people from working-class backgrounds face when navigating elite spaces. Isolation can distort perceptions of success, making it seem both unattainable and exclusive to "others."

Despite these challenges, JD recognized the value of his education and the opportunities it afforded him. Mamaw had always fought to instill in him the belief that he could achieve great things, and for the most part, she succeeded. At Yale, JD learned not just to embrace his differences but also to use them as a source of strength. His story became a bridge, connecting the world he came from with the one he was beginning to thrive in.

The Complexities of Social Mobility

Social mobility often implies progress toward a better life, but it also involves leaving behind parts of one's old identity, creating tension between past and present. This duality became clear to JD during his time at Yale Law School. For him, moving into elite spaces wasn't just about financial improvement; it was about navigating new cultural norms and values that clashed with his upbringing.

He observed how those from upper-class backgrounds viewed people like him as outsiders, such as the professor who questioned accepting students from state schools. This outsider perception isn't easily quantified but plays a role in why many working-class individuals not only struggle to ascend the social ladder but often fall after reaching it. For JD, social mobility meant adopting a lifestyle unfamiliar to his roots, from shopping at Whole Foods to vacationing abroad, while distancing himself from old traditions like enjoying Cracker Barrel with pride.

Yet, these changes came with an underlying question: Why do so few from backgrounds like his break into elite spaces? For JD, the journey revealed that upward mobility is about more than financial success; it's a cultural transformation that requires bridging two worlds and understanding the values of both.

CHAPTER 17

Finding His Place, and Usha

JD Vance's first year at Yale Law School was as much about adjusting to a new world as it was about earning a degree. He was surrounded by a culture that felt foreign, but in the midst of it, he met Usha. Assigned as partners for a writing project, they spent hours working together, and JD couldn't help but admire her. She seemed to embody every positive quality a person could have: intelligent, hardworking, confident, and beautiful. Her honesty set her apart. Where others might soften criticism, Usha was direct. "This sentence doesn't work," she'd say simply, or at a bar, she'd casually tell a friend, "You have a very small head," without a trace of irony. To JD, she was unlike anyone he'd ever met.

Though JD had dated before, nothing compared to how he felt about Usha. His friends teased him, calling him "heartsick," and they weren't wrong. When he found out she was single, he didn't hesitate. After one date, he broke every unspoken rule of modern dating and confessed that he was in love with her. Somehow, it worked.

Usha quickly became more than a romantic partner—she was a guide through the maze of Yale. She encouraged him to embrace opportunities he didn't even know existed. "Go to office hours," she'd say. "Professors here like talking to students. That's part of the experience." With her by his side, JD began to feel like he belonged, at least a little.

This sense of adjustment was tested during Yale's Fall Interview Program, where top law firms courted students for prestigious jobs. JD was invited to a dinner with Gibson, Dunn & Crutcher, one of the firms he most admired. The event was high-stakes, and JD felt the weight of it.

When a waiter asked whether he'd prefer sauvignon blanc or chardonnay, JD froze. He had no idea what sauvignon blanc was but figured it must be a type of white wine. To play it safe, he ordered the chardonnay because it was easier to pronounce. It was a small, ridiculous moment, but it felt like dodging a bullet.

For JD, the night underscored how far he'd come—and how much further he had to go. Yet with Usha's support and his growing confidence, he began to see that he could hold his own in a world that once seemed completely out of reach.

Navigating the World of Elite Job Interviews

JD Vance's introduction to the high-stakes world of elite law firm interviews was nothing short of surreal. He arrived at one of New Haven's fanciest restaurants for a dinner hosted by Gibson, Dunn & Crutcher, a firm he admired. The setting, with its pristine wine glasses, luxurious linens, and sharply dressed attorneys, left him feeling like an outsider.

Though determined to focus on making a good impression, JD couldn't help but get caught up in the spectacle. When the waitress asked if he wanted "tap or sparkling" water, he chose sparkling, assuming it was simply fancier. His first sip, however, revealed that sparkling water was just carbonated water. Mortified, he spit it out and declared something must be wrong with the drink. Thankfully, only a classmate noticed the mishap, and JD resolved to avoid further mistakes.

Next came the minefield of utensils at the table. With nine pieces of silverware in front of him, JD was baffled. He excused himself to the restroom and called Usha, his trusted guide through Yale. Her simple advice—start from the outside and work inward—saved him from potential embarrassment. Returning to the table, he kept his focus on the conversation and followed his sister Lindsay's advice to chew with his mouth closed. By the end of the evening, he managed to make a good impression, landing a coveted follow-up interview.

But the dinner wasn't just about fine dining or fancy settings. It revealed an essential truth about elite professional culture: success wasn't solely about talent or hard work. It was about belonging. Yale Law's career office had emphasized that interviews weren't just about résumés or grades—those were already taken care of by the school's reputation. Instead, interviews were a social test, evaluating whether candidates could thrive in high-pressure boardrooms and fit in with future clients.

The Importance of Networks

JD was struck by how the game was rigged in favor of those with social capital. He marveled at how easily his classmates accessed prestigious opportunities. All week, he and his peers glided through interview after interview, many of which led to six-figure job offers. Just a few years earlier, he had struggled to find any decent post-college job, sending out dozens of résumés without much success. Now, Yale's reputation had opened doors that previously felt bolted shut.

The process revealed how much value networks bring. Successful candidates didn't rely solely on résumés or job applications; they leaned on professors, family connections, and institutional prestige to pave their way. JD had always thought finding a job meant cold applications and hoping for a callback. But here, success depended on knowing the right people and navigating hidden systems.

That realization came into sharp focus during one of his final interviews of the week. By then, JD had polished his responses and mastered the dance of discussing firm culture and work-life balance. But when an interviewer asked why he wanted to work at a law firm, he fumbled. Instead of delivering a professional answer about learning from the best, JD blurted out, "I don't really know, but the pay isn't bad! Ha ha!"

The interviewer's blank stare confirmed his worst fears: he had blown it. JD left the interview certain he'd failed. But behind the scenes, a Yale professor who had recommended him was working the phones, vouching for him to the hiring partner. "She raved about you," he later learned. Despite his misstep, JD got the callback and eventually the job offer.

This experience hammered home another lesson: having the right network could sometimes compensate for being less polished. While talent and effort mattered, knowing someone willing to advocate for you often mattered more. JD realized that the rules of success he'd learned growing up—hard work and perseverance—were only part of the equation. Social capital, connections, and institutional backing were equally, if not more, important.

By the end of that grueling week, JD had a clearer understanding of how the elite world operated. It wasn't about blindly sending out résumés or working tirelessly in isolation. It was about leveraging relationships and being part of a system that most people never even knew existed. For someone like JD, who had started so far outside that system, it was both an eye-opening and humbling revelation.

CHAPTER 18

Learning to Navigate the Labyrinth of Success

At Yale Law, networking wasn't just a buzzword—it was an unspoken currency that seemed to flow effortlessly among certain students, leaving others to catch up. For JD, the writing competition for *The Yale Law Journal* epitomized this divide. Membership on the Journal was a golden ticket in the legal world, opening doors to prestigious clerkships and jobs. It seemed like everyone had a strategy, often shaped by networks of alumni, professors, and friends. Some students had started preparing months in advance, guided by insider tips from those who had already climbed the ladder.

JD, however, had no such roadmap. Coming from Ohio State, he had no alumni network to rely on and little understanding of why the Journal mattered so much. The mixed messages from official channels didn't help. Professors downplayed its importance, saying it wasn't essential for all career paths, but they also acknowledged that it was crucial for certain high-powered jobs. Lost in the confusion, JD turned to Professor Amy Chua, whose candid advice provided clarity.

"If you want to clerk or pursue academia, it's worth it," she told him. "Otherwise, it's not. But if you're unsure, give it a shot." That advice transformed what had felt like a mystery into a manageable choice. Though he didn't make it his first year, JD earned a spot the next year and became an editor. What mattered more than the result, though, was the process of learning how to close the information gap.

Finding Value Beyond Credentials

The Journal experience was just one of many decisions JD faced in law school. Another came with the question of judicial clerkships. Clerkships are coveted positions with federal judges that offer young lawyers a front-row seat to the legal system. They're prestigious, provide invaluable experience, and often come with lucrative bonuses when transitioning to private-sector jobs.

JD knew the basics but quickly realized how much more there was to understand. Clerkships varied by court type—trial or appellate—and by location. Some judges, known as "feeders," could virtually guarantee a Supreme Court clerkship, but they were notoriously selective. Others were known for being difficult to work with. The process of choosing a judge was as much about politics and personalities as it was about credentials.

To navigate this labyrinth, JD relied on Amy Chua again. She warned him against pursuing a feeder judge. "If you don't want to be a Supreme Court litigator, you don't need this credential," she said. But JD couldn't shake the idea of the prestige. Eventually, she agreed to recommend him to a high-powered federal judge with strong connections to the Supreme Court.

JD submitted his materials, unsure of why he was chasing the opportunity. Perhaps it was a desire to prove himself, to silence the nagging doubts that he didn't belong at Yale. When Amy called to tell him he'd made the judge's short list, his excitement was tempered by her sobering words: "You're doing this for the wrong reasons."

She explained that the judge's demanding nature would leave no room for anything else in his life—not even a single day off during the yearlong clerkship. Then she added something more personal: "This kind of job destroys relationships. You have Usha now. Don't sacrifice her for a credential that doesn't serve your goals."

Amy's advice hit home. JD asked her to withdraw his application. It wasn't an easy decision, but it was the right one. He didn't need the validation of an ultra-prestigious clerkship to prove his worth. Instead, he chose to focus on the life and career he truly wanted, not the one others expected him to pursue.

The experience was a turning point. It taught JD that success wasn't about following a preordained path but about making choices aligned with his values and goals. Amy's guidance wasn't just professional— it was deeply personal. She gave him permission to prioritize his relationship with Usha and to define success on his own terms.

This moment underscored the profound value of social capital—not just in opening doors but in offering wisdom. JD had learned through his network what he couldn't have discovered on his own: how to weigh options, avoid pitfalls, and stay true to himself.

Social capital isn't just about connections; it's about mentorship, guidance, and learning through others. For JD, Amy's advice was priceless. It wasn't just career-defining; it was life-changing. And it reminded him that sometimes, the best path forward isn't the most prestigious one—it's the one that lets you be your best self.

The Hidden Curriculum of Success

JD's education in social capital didn't end when he entered Yale Law School—it continued to evolve, shaping his career and personal life. While contributing to a website run by journalist David Frum, JD received advice that changed his trajectory. Frum suggested a D.C. law firm where two former Bush administration officials had recently become senior partners. Following this lead, JD landed an interview with one of them, who later became a mentor. That connection eventually brought JD face-to-face with Indiana governor Mitch Daniels, his political hero, at a Yale conference. Without Frum's guidance, these opportunities would have been out of reach.

When JD decided to pursue a judicial clerkship, he approached it with clarity, knowing what he wanted: a meaningful learning experience, respect for his boss, and proximity to Usha. Together, they navigated the clerkship process and found positions in northern Kentucky, near his roots. The experience was so fulfilling that their judicial bosses officiated their wedding—a perfect culmination of professional and personal harmony.

This journey underscored the power of social capital. Those who access it flourish, while those without it face significant hurdles. JD had practically compiled a list of lessons he learned only after he came to Yale—from wearing the right suit to understanding the unspoken rules of professional life.

Mamaw bristled at the hillbilly stereotype, but JD couldn't ignore how much he didn't know. These gaps in knowledge carried real consequences, costing him jobs and opportunities. At Yale, a few mentors bridged those gaps, offering the guidance that kids like him often lack. For JD, the lesson was clear: the difference between sinking and swimming often lies not in ability but in understanding the hidden rules of success.

COPING

'I eventually got to the point where I was like, 'Well, if I can't believe in the Big Bang Theory and be a good Christian, then maybe I'm not a good Christian.'

CHAPTER 19

The Cycle of Instability and
the Struggle to Break Free

As JD entered his second year of law school, everything seemed to be falling into place. He had spent the summer interning at the U.S. Senate, had an amazing girlfriend in Usha, and felt confident about his career prospects. On the surface, he had defied the odds. But beneath the surface, old patterns of behavior and family scars lingered.

Usha's observation about him being a "turtle" hit hard. Whenever conflict arose, JD withdrew, retreating into a shell of avoidance. It wasn't just a quirk; it was deeply ingrained. Growing up in a home where shouting and fleeing were common solutions, he had learned to either lash out or shut down. So, when disagreements with Usha surfaced, JD found himself repeating the very behaviors he despised in his mother.

One moment stood out during a trip to D.C. for law firm interviews. After a particularly rough interview, JD returned to their hotel room frustrated and self-critical. When Usha tried to console him, he exploded, shouting that he didn't get this far by "making excuses for failure." Storming out, he spent hours pacing the streets of D.C., haunted by memories of his family's chaos. He remembered his mom dragging him to a motel after one of her fights with Bob, and his grandmother running with her daughters to escape an alcoholic father. These moments of running away had shaped him, and he realized he was still trying to escape rather than confront problems.

When Usha found him sitting near Ford's Theatre, her calm response to his apology startled him. She didn't lash out or let the argument fester. Instead, she demanded better communication and gave him grace. Her approach was entirely foreign to JD Her family, as he later learned, solved problems with empathy and understanding, not shouting or avoidance.

The Roots of Conflict and Generational Trauma

JD's struggles weren't unique—they were part of a cycle deeply rooted in his upbringing. After trying and failing to connect with a counselor, JD turned to research and learned about adverse childhood experiences (ACEs). These are traumatic events during childhood that leave lasting scars. Being insulted, witnessing violence, growing up with addiction, or experiencing constant instability—these were hallmarks of his youth.

JD wasn't alone. Research showed that people from working-class backgrounds, like his own, were significantly more likely to experience ACEs than their middle- or upper-class counterparts. Four in ten working-class individuals faced multiple childhood traumas, compared to just 29 percent in wealthier demographics. These traumas didn't just fade with time; they left marks on the brain, hardwiring children for constant conflict and stress.

Harvard researchers found that prolonged exposure to stress during childhood could fundamentally alter brain chemistry. The fight-or-flight response, useful in emergencies, became a constant presence. For kids like JD, the "bear" wasn't an occasional threat—it was an alcoholic parent, a volatile household, or the fear of abandonment. Even in adulthood, when the chaos subsided, the wiring for conflict remained.

JD's family instability was a microcosm of a broader issue in working-class America. His mother's revolving door of partners reflected a troubling national trend. One in twelve American children, especially in working-class communities, experienced multiple changes in family structure—a rate far higher than in other developed countries. This instability wasn't just a symptom of economic hardship; it was a cause of further chaos, perpetuating cycles of poverty and dysfunction.

Through Usha, JD glimpsed an alternative. Her family wasn't perfect, but their approach to conflict was a revelation. They emphasized communication and commitment, even with estranged relatives. Her father's comment—"You've got to make the effort, because they're family"—stood in stark contrast to the cycles of blame and avoidance JD had grown up with.

When JD first attempted to visit a counselor, the experience was overwhelming. The mere thought of sharing his feelings with a stranger made him physically uncomfortable, so he turned to books instead. At the library, he discovered that the turmoil he and his sister Lindsay experienced growing up wasn't just anecdotal—it was a well-documented phenomenon called *adverse childhood experiences* (ACEs). This framework gave a name to the chaos he thought was normal, providing a lens through which to examine his life and the lives of those around him.

Understanding the Weight of Childhood Trauma

ACEs cover a spectrum of childhood traumas: verbal abuse, physical aggression, neglect, parental separation, addiction in the home, mental illness, and exposure to domestic violence. While these events can occur in any community, JD learned they were disproportionately common in working-class families like his own. Research supported what he had long felt—that his upbringing was marked by challenges many of his Yale peers couldn't fathom. A study by the Wisconsin Children's Trust Fund showed that over 40 percent of working-class individuals had experienced multiple ACEs, compared to only 29 percent in the upper-middle class and beyond.

JD decided to test this out. Using an ACEs quiz developed by psychologists, he asked his family and Usha to assess their childhoods. The results were stark. Aunt Wee scored a seven, even higher than JD and Lindsay, who both had six. In contrast, Usha and Uncle Dan—people who had grown up in stable, nurturing households—scored a perfect zero. The difference was eye-opening. It wasn't just about individual experiences; it was about systemic, generational cycles of trauma.

The implications of these scores were profound. Children with multiple ACEs are more likely to face mental health challenges, struggle in school, and have unstable relationships as adults. Even their physical health isn't spared: ACEs correlate with higher risks of heart disease, cancer, and obesity. Harvard researchers found that constant stress, like what JD endured as a child, can actually alter brain chemistry, keeping the body in a perpetual fight-or-flight mode. As Dr. Nadine Burke Harris explained, this response is helpful in a life-threatening situation, like encountering a bear in the forest. But when "the bear comes home from the bar every night," the system becomes chronically activated, leaving children hardwired for conflict even when the danger subsides.

CHAPTER 20

Breaking the Cycle

The data was sobering, but it was also empowering. For the first time, JD understood that his responses to stress and conflict weren't just personal failings—they were survival mechanisms ingrained during his chaotic upbringing. Armed with this knowledge, he began to dissect his emotional triggers and confront the patterns he'd inherited.

One of the most powerful revelations came from conversations with his family. Aunt Wee, who had one of the highest ACEs scores in the family, shared how she used to brace herself physically before arguments with her husband, Dan. Even in her happy marriage, she carried the muscle memory of conflict from her youth. "Sometimes I'd stand there like I was ready for a fight," she admitted. Yet her relationship with Dan improved once she realized she didn't always have to be on guard.

Lindsay echoed a similar journey. Early in her marriage, she found herself lashing out at her husband, Kevin, and pushing him away. "When we fought, I'd tell him to just leave, because I thought that's what he wanted anyway," she said. Kevin's bewildered response— "Why do you fight with me like I'm your enemy?"—forced her to confront her defensive instincts. Sixteen years later, Lindsay and Kevin remained married, proving that healing was possible, even for those steeped in family conflict.

For JD, the hardest part was unlearning what he thought were survival skills. He had grown up in an environment where apologies were often manipulative, a prelude to more betrayal or chaos. Lowering his guard felt dangerous. Words, he realized, had always been his most potent weapon, honed in a home where disagreements were battles to win. These habits didn't fade overnight. He described himself as a "delayed explosion," someone who could be defused only with care and patience.

It was in Usha that JD found the patience and stability he needed. Her background, devoid of the instability he had known, offered a stark contrast to his own. Her family didn't fight with insults or silence; they communicated with kindness and honesty. Through her, he began to see the possibility of a different kind of relationship—one built on mutual respect rather than guarded hostility.

But even as he grew, JD couldn't ignore the patterns in his family and community. The chaos and instability weren't just personal—they were cultural. America's working class, particularly in areas like his hometown, experiences family breakdown at an alarming rate. In France, only 0.5 percent of children are exposed to three or more maternal partners. In Sweden, the figure rises slightly to 2.6 percent. In the United States, it's a staggering 8.2 percent, with even higher rates in working-class communities. This instability, sociologists argue, creates a vicious cycle: children exposed to multiple family transitions are more likely to struggle as adults, perpetuating the pattern.

JD saw this play out in his own family. His mother, the salutatorian of her high school, had both a child and a divorce before she turned twenty. His aunt married an abusive man at sixteen to escape a turbulent home. "Out of the frying pan and into the fire" became a grim refrain. Chaos begets chaos, and stability feels like an impossible dream.

Yet there were exceptions—glimmers of hope. JD noticed that the family members who had built stable lives all married outside their culture. Aunt Wee, Lindsay, and even his cousin Gail found partners who brought different values and coping mechanisms to the table. These relationships weren't immune to conflict, but they were grounded in something deeper: a commitment to break the cycle.

For JD, breaking the cycle wasn't just about personal growth—it was about survival. He fought against the odds every day, knowing that the statistics were stacked against him. But he also found solace in small victories: a moment of patience during an argument, a calm discussion instead of a heated fight. These changes, though incremental, signaled a new path forward.

Ultimately, JD understood that his journey wasn't just about escaping his past but learning to live with it. The scars of his childhood would never fully fade, but they didn't have to define him. With Usha by his side and a newfound awareness of his triggers, he began to build a life that felt less like a battle and more like a home.

This realization shook the foundation of JD's self-image. For so long, he had framed his life as a triumph over adversity, a narrative of strength and resilience. He had escaped his troubled hometown, served in the Marines, excelled at Ohio State, and earned a place at Yale Law

School. In his mind, these accomplishments meant he had no demons, no flaws, and no lingering issues from his past. But as he confronted his struggles—especially in building a happy home and relationship—he realized that his self-image was little more than bitterness dressed up as arrogance.

By his second year of law school, JD had cut contact with his mom, a decision he had never previously made. Despite his myriad feelings toward her—love, anger, pity, forgiveness, hatred—he had never considered sympathy. For years, he had categorized her as defective, perhaps even broken in some genetic way, and hoped that he hadn't inherited the same flaws. But as he began to see his mother's behavior mirrored in himself, he found himself trying to understand her.

Uncle Jimmy once shared a memory that stayed with JD In the midst of another crisis with his mom, Mamaw and Papaw sat discussing how they could bail her out—again. Papaw, known for his stoic strength, buried his face in his hands and wept. "I've failed her," he cried over and over. Uncle Jimmy had never seen Papaw cry before. It was a rare moment of vulnerability, but it brought up an uncomfortable question: How much of life's trajectory is shaped by personal decisions, and how much is inherited from family and culture? Where does personal responsibility end, and where does sympathy begin?

The family had varying opinions. Uncle Jimmy rejected the idea that any of Mom's struggles were Papaw's fault. "It's her own damned fault," he insisted. Aunt Wee, who had faced similar challenges in the same household, agreed. Having overcome her own mistakes, she believed Mom should have been able to do the same. Lindsay, on the other hand, had a bit more sympathy. She believed their upbringing had left them all with demons and that Mom's childhood likely haunted her in ways similar to their own. But even Lindsay drew a line. "At some point," she said, "you have to stop making excuses and take responsibility."

JD found himself caught in the middle. On one hand, the constant fighting and alcoholism that marked their childhood must have taken a toll on Mom. He saw how, even as children, his mom and her siblings responded to conflict differently. While Aunt Wee confronted the chaos head-on, Mom would hide, run, or shut down. In some ways, JD believed, Mom was the sibling who lost the statistical game of their upbringing. But he also knew that no one—himself included—gets a free pass for their childhood. Love and effort weren't enough if they weren't accompanied by accountability.

Mom's influence had always been a source of intense emotions for JD As a child, he adored her fiercely, defending her honor in kindergarten by punching a classmate who insulted her umbrella. But her repeated battles with addiction often left him filled with anger and resentment. At his darkest moments, he wished she would disappear entirely, freeing him and Lindsay from her chaos. Yet there were also moments of tenderness, like when she lay sobbing in bed after another failed relationship, leaving JD consumed with rage at her suffering and the forces that had caused it.

Toward the end of his law school journey, Lindsay called to share that Mom had started using heroin and was trying rehab again. It shouldn't have surprised him—Mom had cycled through rehab and hospital stays many times before—but the word "heroin" carried a certain gravity. To him, it was the apex of all drugs, a final and devastating frontier. A cloud of despair hung over him for weeks. It wasn't hatred or anger he felt anymore but fear: fear for her safety, fear for Lindsay, and fear for himself. Was he really any different? Could he truly escape the cycle of addiction and instability? Graduating from Yale Law should have made him feel invincible, but instead, he found himself questioning whether people like him could ever truly change.

When JD graduated, eighteen family members came to celebrate, including cousins Denise and Gail, as well as Usha's family, who met his for the first time. The gathering was joyful, even if Denise offered some blunt critiques of the modern art at the museum they visited. Mom, however, didn't make the trip. At that moment, she wasn't using drugs, and JD took that as a small victory. He didn't expect more.

Justice Sonia Sotomayor delivered the commencement address, reassuring the graduates that it was okay to be unsure about their future paths. For JD, her words carried a deeper significance. He had learned much about the law at Yale, but more importantly, he had come to understand himself and his place in the world. He realized that his new life—so far removed from Middletown—would always feel a little foreign. Being a hillbilly meant carrying the weight of both love and war, often indistinguishable from one another. As he walked across the stage, he felt pride in his achievements but also uncertainty about the path ahead. Could he reconcile the pieces of his past with the person he was becoming? That was the question that lingered most.

CHAPTER 21

The memory of that night at the roadside motel stays etched in his mind, especially the spiders—huge, looming creatures like something out of a nightmare. Standing outside the dingy office, separated by a pane of glass from the disheveled woman behind the counter, JD noticed the webs strung between the building and a makeshift sunshade. Each one held at least one enormous spider, and though he wasn't normally afraid of them, their sheer size unnerved him. He couldn't shake the feeling that if he looked away for even a second, one of those grotesque creatures would pounce.

This wasn't where JD imagined himself, not after structuring his entire life to escape places like this. Yet there he was, well past midnight, staring at a hypodermic needle dangling from a man's arm as he slouched half out of his truck nearby. It wasn't even shocking—this was Middletown, after all. Just weeks earlier, the police had found a woman unconscious at a car wash, heroin and a spoon beside her, the needle still in her arm.

The motel clerk looked older than her years, her gray, greasy hair framing a face worn down by life. Her meek, childlike voice was barely audible as she struggled to process JD's credit card on an ancient swipe machine. "People usually pay cash," she explained apologetically. When she handed the card back, her eyes pleaded silently, like she was trapped in her own life. "Enjoy your stay," she said, even though JD had told her earlier the room wasn't for him but for his homeless mother.

It was a surreal moment. Just months earlier, JD had graduated from Yale Law School and married Usha in a beautiful ceremony in Kentucky, surrounded by family. He had everything—an impressive job, a new home in Cincinnati, two dogs, and a seemingly perfect life. On the surface, he had achieved the American Dream. But that night was a stark reminder that upward mobility is rarely tidy. The past, no matter how far you run, has a way of catching up.

JD didn't know all the details of how his mother had ended up homeless, but he knew enough. Her latest husband—number five—had kicked her out after she stole family heirlooms to buy prescription drugs. Their marriage was over, and she had nowhere to go. JD had vowed years ago never to help his mother again. But the man who made that promise had changed. He was now exploring a faith he had abandoned long ago and had learned the full extent of his mother's childhood trauma. Those wounds, he realized, didn't just disappear. They lingered, for her and for him.

So when he got the call about her dire situation, he didn't hang up in anger. Instead, he offered to help. He had called a Middletown motel, intending to pay for a week's stay with his credit card, but they wouldn't accept payment over the phone. That's how he found himself driving from Cincinnati at 11 PM on a Tuesday, determined to keep his mom off the streets.

JD's plan was simple: give his mom enough support to get back on her feet. She'd find her own place, save money, and work toward reinstating her nursing license. In the meantime, he'd monitor her finances to ensure she stayed clean. It reminded him of the plans Mamaw and Papaw used to concoct, full of hope but destined to fail. Still, he convinced himself this time would be different.

But helping his mom wasn't as straightforward as he hoped. The motel, with its grim surroundings and eerie silence, filled him with a deep unease. The practicalities of managing her finances were even more draining. The emotional weight of trying to help someone who often seemed beyond saving was heavier than he'd anticipated.

Through it all, JD wrestled with his conflicting emotions. He had learned to see his mom not as a villain but as a deeply flawed person scarred by her own past. She had tried to be a good mother and had moments of success, but her life was a series of poor choices and missed opportunities. JD could forgive her for some of it, but not all. No one, not even his mother, gets an endless free pass for their mistakes.

Over time, JD found a balance. He no longer avoided his mother out of anger or fear, but he also understood his limits. He could offer help when he had the emotional and financial resources to do so, but he wouldn't let her needs jeopardize his own well-being or the happiness of his family. It was an uneasy truce, one born of both love and self-preservation. For now, it worked.

That night at the motel, as he handed over his credit card and prepared to leave, JD knew that the cycle wasn't broken. He might never fully escape the pull of his past or the pain of his mother's struggles. But he also knew that helping her, even in small ways, was part of what made him who he was. It was a reminder that the American Dream, no matter how shiny it looks, often comes with complicated baggage.

CHAPTER 22

The Weight of a Helping Hand

People often ask JD if he believes there's a solution to the challenges facing his community. They're hoping for a clear, actionable answer—a government policy or a public initiative that could neatly solve the problems of Appalachia. But JD doesn't see it that way. The issues of family, faith, and culture are complex and deeply ingrained, not problems that can be "fixed" like a broken Rubik's Cube. A friend of his, someone who once worked in the White House, put it best: "You probably can't fix these things. But maybe you can put your thumb on the scale for people at the margins."

For JD, those thumbs on the scale were numerous, small interventions at just the right time. His grandparents, Mamaw and Papaw, were his constant anchor, even when his mother and stepfather tried to push them away. Though his family life was a revolving door of father figures, JD was lucky to be surrounded by a few kind and caring men. His sister, Lindsay, always protected him. Teachers, distant relatives, and friends all played their part. Without any one of these supports, he knows he might not have made it.

JD's story is not unique. Others who have beaten the odds point to similar experiences. A friend, Jane Rex, who now helps transfer students at Appalachian State University, talks about the stable family that empowered her and the exposure to a broader world that gave her something to dream for. Her friend's father, a bank president, showed her a life she might not have known existed. Seeing it made her believe it was possible.

Stories of Resilience

JD's cousin Gail lived a life that many would call the American Dream: a beautiful home, three children, a loving marriage, and a personality that radiated kindness. She was often called the "nicest person in the world," and it was a title she fully deserved. But Gail's journey wasn't free of adversity. At just seven years old, her father left. By seventeen, her mother issued an ultimatum: break up with her boyfriend or forget about college. Gail moved out the day after her high school graduation and found herself pregnant by August.

Her life unraveled quickly. Family members turned their backs when they learned she was having a biracial child. Arguments escalated, and Gail became estranged from her relatives. Despite these challenges, she refused to crumble. Gail's daughter became her identity, and she imposed strict rules on herself: no drugs, no alcohol, and nothing that might jeopardize her child's safety. She found a job, worked her way up, returned to school, and eventually remarried. Her second marriage, to Allan, brought her the fairy tale ending she had worked so hard to achieve.

Gail's story mirrored those of many in JD's world: teenagers placed in impossible situations, often of their own making but sometimes not. The odds were stacked against them. Some succumbed to crime or addiction, but others, like Gail, found ways to push through. They drew strength from family, mentors, or a vision of what was possible.

A groundbreaking study by economist Raj Chetty highlighted the disparities in opportunity across the United States. Poor children in places like Utah, Oklahoma, and Massachusetts had better chances of climbing the economic ladder than those in Appalachia or the Rust Belt. Chetty identified two critical factors in these disparities: the prevalence of single-parent households and income segregation. Growing up in neighborhoods dominated by poverty and fractured families significantly narrowed the realm of possibilities. Without someone to guide and inspire them, many children never saw a way out.

JD wasn't surprised by these findings. In his world, the presence of a Mamaw and Papaw or a mentor who opened doors often marked the difference between success and failure. Mormon Utah, with its strong sense of community, intact families, and integrated neighborhoods, stood in sharp contrast to the fragmented, isolated world of Rust Belt Ohio. For JD, Gail's story embodied resilience, determination, and the critical role that family and community could play in transforming lives.

The Role of Policy and Informal Interventions

JD believed there are lessons to be learned from his experiences, even if they don't fit the mold of traditional public policy. Social services systems, for example, could be more responsive to families like his. When JD's mother was arrested, the social workers were ostensibly there to protect him. But they were often obstacles, insisting that the courts might not allow him to stay with Mamaw because she wasn't a licensed foster parent. The threat of being placed with strangers terrified JD, so he lied to the social workers, insisting everything was fine.

In the end, JD was able to stay with Mamaw, but the arrangement was entirely informal. It worked because Mamaw was a force of nature, willing to do whatever it took to keep her family together. Not every family had a Mamaw, and JD knew how lucky he was to have someone who fought so fiercely for him.

JD's story underscored the importance of small interventions— mentors, stable role models, and glimpses of a better life. These weren't solutions in the traditional sense, but they were ways to put a thumb on the scale for kids on the margins. They show that success wasn't just about pulling yourself up by your bootstraps; sometimes, it was about having someone there to steady you as you try.

The Complexities of Hillbilly Survival

Not everyone has the safety net of a formidable hillbilly like Mamaw, and for many children in struggling families, state child services represented the last buffer before a complete collapse. Yet these systems were not built with families like JD's in mind. In many communities, extended family networks—grandparents, aunts, uncles—play critical roles, yet state laws often exclude them. In JD's case, social workers viewed his grandmother as an unqualified caretaker because she didn't hold the proper foster license. This bureaucratic rigidity often worsened an already dire situation. The result? A social services system that inadvertently cut off the lifelines for the very children it is supposed to protect.

This issue wasn't small. Each year, 640,000 children entered foster care in the United States, most from low-income families. Added to this the countless children who suffer abuse or neglect but never enter the system, and it became clear that this was a nationwide epidemic. Policies that alienated extended family members from caregiving roles only exacerbated the crisis.

CHAPTER 23

The Need for Early and Meaningful Interventions

JD's experiences suggested that interventions needed to come earlier in a child's life. During a conversation with teachers from his alma mater, Middletown High, they voiced a common frustration: society often focused its resources too late. One teacher observed, "It's like our politicians think college is the only way. For many, it's great. But a lot of our kids have no realistic shot at getting a college degree." Another teacher shared a heartbreaking story about a student who had "lost her baby like she'd lost her car keys." This young mother's child was later found in New York City with the father, a drug dealer, and his family. These cases reflected the deep-rooted chaos in these children's lives—chaos that no amount of late-game policy could fully address.

One potential fix, as a teacher suggested, was rethinking how Section 8 housing vouchers were allocated. Too often, these vouchers concentrated low-income families in isolated, resource-deprived neighborhoods. This segregation created what one teacher called a "bigger pool of hopelessness." Instead, integrating these families into more socioeconomically diverse neighborhoods could have exposed children to role models and alternative lifestyles, offering them a broader view of what was possible. Yet efforts to implement such changes in Middletown faced resistance from federal agencies, which preferred the status quo of clustered poverty.

The Cultural Challenges of Education and Identity

Some obstacles, however, couldn't be solved by policy alone. In JD's world, academic success was often dismissed as unmanly. Boys who excelled in school were labeled "sissies" or worse. This cultural attitude wasn't unique to Appalachia; research showed that working-class boys across the U.S. underperformed in school partly because they viewed academic achievement as feminine. This mentality, deeply ingrained in communities like JD's, couldn't be undone by a government program or a new law. It required a cultural shift that was much harder to legislate.

This clash between survival instincts and success extended into adulthood. JD acknowledged that many traits he developed to endure his chaotic upbringing later hindered his ability to thrive. For example, as a child, hiding money in multiple places was a survival strategy to prevent theft. As an adult, this habit translated into poor financial management and multiple bank accounts with past-due balances. Similarly, the combative mindset that once protected him—whether from bullies at school or threats at home—didn't serve him well in professional or personal relationships.

Breaking the Cycle of Honor and Conflict

One of JD's most vivid realizations of this came during a car ride in Cincinnati. When another driver cut him off and flipped him off, his first instinct was to jump out of the car and demand an apology. He even unbuckled his seatbelt and opened the door before thinking better of it and staying in his seat. His wife, Usha, praised him for resisting his "natural instinct," but JD struggled to see it as a victory. For most of his life, standing down in a situation like that would have labeled him a coward—a "pussy" or a "wimp." Honor, instilled in him from childhood, had been a shield against the chaos of his environment. To back down felt like a betrayal of everything that had once kept him safe.

This tension between old instincts and new realities was a constant battle. In his childhood, honor had meant everything: protecting his family, standing up to bullies, and maintaining a sense of control in an unpredictable world. But as an adult, honor could quickly turn destructive, leading to unnecessary conflict or, worse, legal trouble. The fact that he managed to stay in the car that day was progress, but it didn't come easily. Even hours later, he silently berated himself for not confronting the other driver.

Finding a Middle Ground

JD acknowledged that he couldn't fully escape the influences of his upbringing, nor did he need to. The survival skills he developed as a child had their place, but they required recalibration. His wife, Usha, often reminded him that not every perceived slight warranted a reaction, and over time, he learned to trust her judgment. However, the emotional scars from his past remained. The lessons of his childhood—about conflict, trust, and honor—didn't disappear overnight.

The uneasy truce JD struck with himself involved balancing his instincts with the needs of his current life. He recognized that helping his community required more than just pointing fingers at government policies. It meant addressing the deeply embedded cultural norms and systemic barriers that kept families like his stuck. It also meant acknowledging that change was a slow, often imperfect process. For JD, that was progress. It was the realization that survival and success were not mutually exclusive but required constant adjustment. And sometimes, the greatest victory was simply staying in the car.

CHAPTER 24

The Turning Point: Peter Thiel's Influence

In 2011, during his time at Yale Law School, JD JD attended a talk by Peter Thiel, a venture capitalist and co-founder of PayPal, who was then more known in Silicon Valley circles than in mainstream media. JD had no particular expectations going into the talk, but what he heard profoundly altered his perspective on success, achievement, and purpose.

Thiel spoke about the increasingly competitive and hierarchical world of elite professionals, where achievement often seemed more about social status than meaningful accomplishment. He critiqued the cutthroat nature of modern professional paths, where people competed endlessly for higher stakes with diminishing rewards—elite clerkships, partnerships at top law firms, and prestigious but ultimately hollow accolades. Thiel juxtaposed this with the stagnation of technological innovation, lamenting that while society had improved communication through platforms like Facebook and Twitter, it had made little progress in areas like transportation, medical cures, or sustainable energy.

For JD, this critique resonated deeply. He realized that his own ambitions were rooted in a race for status rather than a desire for meaningful work. He had been striving for prestigious clerkships and legal jobs without fully understanding why. Thiel's talk articulated something JD had felt but never fully grasped: his obsession with achievement had little to do with purpose or character and everything to do with conforming to an unexamined societal template.

Thiel's words were transformative. They inspired JD to rethink his career trajectory entirely, leading him to leave legal practice after less than two years and pursue a different path in venture capital. But Thiel's influence extended beyond career advice. He also embodied a paradox that challenged JD's assumptions: Thiel was both a brilliant thinker and a practicing Christian. This contradicted the social framework JD had built for himself—one in which intellectual sophistication and faith were mutually exclusive.

Rediscovering Faith Through René Girard

Thiel's openness about his Christianity piqued JD's curiosity, prompting him to explore the philosopher René Girard, under whom Thiel had studied at Stanford. Girard's theories about mimetic desire and scapegoating became a critical lens through which JD began to reevaluate his own beliefs and behaviors.

Girard's idea of mimetic rivalry—the notion that human desires are not intrinsic but shaped by what others want—helped JD understand the pressures he felt at Yale and in elite professional circles. But it was Girard's exploration of scapegoating that had the most profound effect on JD. Girard argued that human civilizations often unify themselves through acts of violence against a scapegoat, who is blamed for societal problems. In Christianity, however, this pattern is reversed: Christ, the ultimate scapegoat, is revealed as innocent, forcing humanity to confront its collective guilt.

This interpretation of Christianity as a critique of humanity's tendency to project its flaws onto others resonated with JD It mirrored the behavior he observed in his generation, particularly in the realm of social media, where people often ganged up on perceived wrongdoers while ignoring their own shortcomings. Girard's insights also made JD reflect on his own life, including his relationships and priorities. He began to see the importance of shifting from external blame to internal accountability.

Writing *Hillbilly Elegy*: A Journey of Reflection

Thiel's influence and Girard's ideas were the backdrop to another significant development in JD's life: the writing of *Hillbilly Elegy*, his memoir that would later become a cultural phenomenon. What began as a personal project evolved into a broader exploration of the social and cultural forces that shaped his life and the lives of others in his community.

When JD started writing in 2013, his tone was often angry and self-assured. He felt resentment toward his mother and a strong conviction in his own abilities. But as he delved deeper into his story, his perspective shifted. By the time the book was published in 2016, JD had developed a more nuanced understanding of the interplay between personal responsibility and systemic challenges.

The writing process forced JD to grapple with questions about the root causes of the problems he witnessed in his Appalachian community. He found that both the left and the right offered incomplete narratives. Conservatives emphasized personal responsibility and cultural dysfunction, often dismissing the systemic barriers that made upward mobility difficult. Liberals, on the other hand, focused on structural inequalities but sometimes framed individuals as passive victims of their circumstances. JD believed the truth lay somewhere in between: people are shaped by their environments, but they also have the agency to make choices within those constraints.

Lessons from Silicon Valley

After leaving law practice, JD moved to Silicon Valley, where he worked in venture capital. His time in the tech industry reinforced many of the insights he had gained from Thiel's talk and Girard's philosophy. Silicon Valley was a world driven by innovation, but it was also a place where success was often measured in terms of wealth and influence rather than societal impact. JD admired the entrepreneurial spirit of the region but remained critical of its insular culture and its emphasis on superficial metrics of success.

In Silicon Valley, JD learned the value of risk-taking and problem-solving—qualities that contrasted sharply with the risk-averse, competitive culture of elite law. He saw how tech entrepreneurs prioritized experimentation and innovation over rigid career paths, a mindset that aligned with his evolving view of work and achievement. At the same time, he was struck by the lack of connection between Silicon Valley's wealth and the struggles of communities like his own.

As JD worked on *Hillbilly Elegy* and immersed himself in the world of venture capital, he found himself straddling two very different worlds: the Appalachian culture of his upbringing and the elite circles of Silicon Valley and Yale. This dual perspective became one of the defining themes of his memoir. JD sought to explain the cultural challenges faced by working-class Americans, including the erosion of social capital, the rise of addiction, and the decline of stable family structures.

He also reflected on his own journey, acknowledging the role of both personal choices and external interventions in his success. His grandparents' love and discipline, the opportunities provided by the military and education, and the mentorship of people like Thiel all played a part in shaping his trajectory.

The Polarized Reception

When *Hillbilly Elegy* hit the shelves, it sparked a whirlwind of praise and critique, reflecting the deeply divided cultural and political climate. For JD, the book was a personal exploration of his roots, but its reception catapulted it into a broader conversation about the white working class in America.

The *New York Times* described the book as "a compassionate, discerning sociological analysis of the white underclass that has helped drive the politics of rebellion, particularly the ascent of Donald J. Trump." For JD, this acknowledgment underscored the book's resonance with readers trying to understand the societal shifts behind Trump's rise. The review highlighted how JD had not only recounted his life but also shed light on the larger struggles of a community often overlooked in mainstream narratives.

At the same time, *The American Conservative* praised JD's memoir as "a powerful new memoir [that] uncovers an America many do not see." This endorsement reflected the book's appeal to a more conservative audience, one that recognized the challenges facing working-class families and valued JD's candid reflections on personal responsibility and resilience. For JD, this kind of response validated his effort to bring his community's struggles to the forefront of national discourse.

However, not all responses were positive. *The New Republic* dismissed the memoir as "little more than a list of myths about welfare queens repackaged as a primer on the white working class." This critique framed JD's narrative as perpetuating harmful stereotypes about poverty and class. For JD, such criticisms likely stung, as his intent was to share a deeply personal story rather than to offer a definitive sociological or political treatise.

The contrasting reviews revealed the complexities of JD's work. While some saw it as a bridge to understanding forgotten communities, others viewed it as a divisive text reinforcing outdated ideas. This polarized reception mirrored the broader divisions in American society, with JD's memoir positioned at the intersection of personal storytelling and political commentary.

CAREER

'I never wanted to be a public intellectual or a talking head.'

CHAPTER 25

Beyond the Memoir

After leaving his brief legal career, JD entered Silicon Valley as a venture capitalist, a move that seemed unorthodox for someone from his background. His entry into the tech world came through connections like Peter Thiel, who had not only inspired him during his time at Yale but also introduced him to the venture capital ecosystem. JD joined Mithril Capital Management, a venture capital firm co-founded by Thiel, which focused on long-term investments in transformative technology and industries. His time at Mithril deepened his understanding of how the tech industry operated and allowed him to engage directly with the innovative yet often insular world of Silicon Valley.

In his work as a venture capitalist, JD explored a wide range of investment opportunities, particularly in fields that aligned with his personal interests and Thiel's philosophy of prioritizing transformative technologies. While he respected the advances made in software and consumer tech, JD often spoke about the need to focus on deeper, systemic innovation—such as advancements in healthcare, energy, and biotechnology. These were areas he believed could meaningfully improve lives, including those of people in struggling communities like the one he came from.

At Mithril, JD worked on identifying companies that weren't merely chasing quick financial returns but had the potential to create long-term societal value. This focus on innovation complemented his personal mission to bridge the gap between the elites of Silicon Valley and the forgotten working-class communities of America. He saw his role as more than just finding promising startups; he wanted to push for investment in companies that addressed real-world problems, including those affecting the economically and socially marginalized.

One of the defining features of JD's time in Silicon Valley was his growing awareness of the cultural disconnect between the tech industry and the rest of the country. Silicon Valley's focus on disruption and rapid scalability often seemed detached from the daily struggles of ordinary Americans. JD was particularly critical of what he perceived as a lack of attention to how technological adjustments impacted jobs and communities outside urban innovation hubs. For example, while tech giants created new efficiencies in logistics and retail, they also displaced traditional jobs in sectors like manufacturing and service industries—jobs that were crucial for working-class families in regions like Appalachia and the Rust Belt.

This awareness spurred JD to think about ways to bring the benefits of innovation to places far removed from Silicon Valley. He began to advocate for decentralizing technology and investing in regions that had been left behind by the tech-driven economy. This vision eventually led to the founding of his own venture capital fund, Narya Capital, in 2020. Named after one of the mythical rings of power in *The Lord of the Rings*, Narya aimed to invest in companies that could thrive outside traditional tech hubs, focusing on startups in industries like healthcare, manufacturing, and agriculture.

JD's time in Silicon Valley thus became a springboard for his broader mission: to reconnect the engines of innovation with the needs of struggling American communities. It also informed his political ambitions, as he sought to use his platform to advocate for policies that would bridge the divide between urban elites and rural America. His work in Silicon Valley was not just a career move but a pivotal chapter in his evolving understanding of the challenges facing modern America and the potential solutions rooted in both innovation and cultural renewal.

A New Vision

Ultimately, JD's experiences in Silicon Valley and his reflections on faith and culture led him to advocate for a more holistic approach to addressing societal problems. He believed that true progress required balancing structural reforms with a revival of personal responsibility and moral accountability. While he remained skeptical of simplistic solutions, he saw hope in efforts to rebuild social capital and create opportunities for upward mobility.

By the time *Hillbilly Elegy* was published, JD had emerged as a unique voice in American discourse—one that bridged the gap between Appalachia and Silicon Valley, between tradition and modernity, and between individual agency and systemic change. His time in Silicon Valley was not just a detour from his legal career; it was a transformative chapter that helped him redefine his purpose and articulate a vision for a better future.

JD often felt a pull back to Ohio, the place that shaped him, even as he built a life far away in Silicon Valley. From the moment he left to join the military, there was always a lingering sense that he wasn't quite finished with his home state. Now, with the success of *Hillbilly Elegy*, JD found himself with the platform, flexibility, and resources to finally act on that desire. It wasn't just nostalgia drawing him back—it was a sense of responsibility to tackle some of the deeply rooted issues he'd witnessed growing up, especially the opioid crisis.

Ohio's grim distinction as a leader in drug overdose deaths struck close to home for JD Addiction wasn't an abstract policy issue for him—it was personal. It ran through the veins of his community and even his own family, leaving scars and struggles he knew too well. Writing his book had forced him to confront those realities, and the book's reception offered him a chance to do more than reflect. It gave him a voice, a platform, and perhaps even the obligation to try to make a difference.

JD's plan wasn't to swoop in with all the answers; he knew better than that. He decided to start small with a nonprofit focused on addressing addiction and other community challenges. His approach was rooted in humility and curiosity—a "listening tour," as he called it, to learn directly from those living the crisis every day. He wanted to hear what people thought might work, what had already been tried, and where the gaps remained. For JD, solutions couldn't come solely from academic research or policy think tanks—they had to come from the people on the ground, grappling with the crisis in their own lives.

His vision wasn't about imposing top-down fixes. Instead, he saw value in grassroots efforts already underway—work happening in churches, community centers, and local organizations. Maybe the answer was expanding access to anti-opioid medications, or maybe it was scaling up successful local initiatives to a statewide level. JD didn't pretend to have all the answers, and he was open about that uncertainty. For him, admitting the complexity of the problem and the need for humility in tackling it was the first step toward meaningful change.

While he acknowledged the enormity of the opioid crisis, JD also saw it as a symbol of the broader struggles facing his community. Addiction wasn't just a personal failure or a lack of willpower; it was tied to economic despair, the collapse of stable industries, and a culture struggling to find its footing in a rapidly changing world. Addressing the crisis, in his mind, also meant rebuilding a sense of hope and opportunity in places like Ohio.

By returning home, JD wasn't just reconnecting with his roots—he was trying to bridge two worlds: the elite circles he had joined and the struggling community he had left. He wanted to use the resources and connections he'd gained to put a "thumb on the scale," as he called it, for the people on the margins. It was a daunting task, and he didn't claim to have all the answers. But he was ready to listen, learn, and do what he could to help. For JD, going back to Ohio wasn't just a personal journey—it was a chance to give back to the place and people who had shaped him.

CHAPTER 26

Path to Politics

The phone wouldn't stop ringing.

JD Vance's path to considering a U.S. Senate run in Ohio was anything but conventional, much like his life up to that point. Fresh off the success of *Hillbilly Elegy*, JD found himself at the center of a political conversation he hadn't entirely sought out. But when Josh Mandel, the GOP frontrunner for the Ohio Senate seat, abruptly withdrew due to a family health issue, a cascade of events brought JD to the brink of candidacy.

The calls started almost immediately. Republican donors, leaders, and strategists reached out, urging JD to reconsider the Senate bid he had earlier dismissed. His adviser, Jai Chabria, described the flood of encouragement as overwhelming. Key figures, including Senate Majority Leader Mitch McConnell, expressed their belief in JD's potential to not only unite the Republican Party in Ohio but to challenge and possibly defeat the Democratic incumbent, Sherrod Brown.

For JD, the decision wasn't simple. He had recently returned to Ohio, focusing on policy issues close to his heart, including the opioid crisis, and building a life with his family after years in Silicon Valley. He knew that entering the political arena would come with scrutiny, especially given his past criticisms of then-presidential candidate Donald Trump. During the 2016 election, JD had openly voiced his concerns about Trump's rhetoric, voting for independent candidate Evan McMullin instead. He questioned whether Trump's approach aligned with the broader, inclusive vision of conservatism he believed in.

That history didn't go unnoticed. Critics within the GOP pointed to JD's reluctance to support Trump as a potential liability in a state the former president had won handily. Meanwhile, others within the party, including McConnell, saw in JD a unique blend of personal experience, intellectual rigor, and a compelling narrative that could resonate deeply with Ohio voters. His book had become a cultural touchstone, viewed by many as a window into the mindset of the very voters who propelled Trump to victory.

As JD weighed his options, the race continued to evolve. U.S. Representative Jim Renacci, who had been running for governor, hinted at switching to the Senate race if Trump supported him, and investment banker Mike Gibbons, a staunch Trump ally, remained a formidable contender. Still, JD's name stood out. His story—one of hardship, perseverance, and eventual success—gave him a rare authenticity that few politicians could claim.

JD approached the prospect of running with a mix of humility and determination. He didn't have all the answers, and he wasn't a career politician. But he recognized the platform his memoir had given him and the responsibility that came with it. He also knew the challenges ahead—bridging the gap between his criticisms of Trump and the loyalty many Ohio Republicans felt toward the former president, and proving that he wasn't just a best-selling author but a candidate capable of navigating the political trenches.

The decision wasn't just about politics for JD; it was about Ohio. He saw the campaign as a chance to bring attention to the struggles of communities like the one he came from and to fight for policies that could make a tangible difference. Whether he would officially enter the race remained uncertain at the time, but one thing was clear: JD wasn't done shaping the conversation in Ohio—or the nation.

JDon Donald Trump

In 2016, JD Vance's views on Donald Trump revealed a complex mix of skepticism and frustration, particularly with the rhetoric and messaging that Trump employed during his campaign. At the time, JD was not yet involved in politics but had become a prominent voice following the success of *Hillbilly Elegy*. He often used that platform to critique what he saw as the shortcomings of Trump's approach to conservatism and its implications for the broader electorate.

JD's concerns centered on Trump's divisive language and its impact on key voting blocs. In a 2016 interview with *Cleveland.com*, he remarked, "He used rhetoric that's not in the best interest of the party or the country. The message of Trump's campaign was obviously not super-appealing to Latino Americans, Black Americans, and so forth. That really bothered me." These comments highlighted JD's belief that conservatism could and should be applied in a way that uplifted all Americans, a vision he felt was undermined by Trump's polarizing tactics.

On social media, JD was equally candid. In a now-deleted tweet from October 2016, he referred to Trump as "reprehensible" and expressed disappointment that so many in the Republican Party were rallying around him. In another tweet from the same period, JD criticized what he called "vulgarity" in Trump's approach, saying that it failed to address the root causes of economic and social struggles faced by working-class communities.

Despite his sharp critiques, JD's position was nuanced. He recognized that Trump had tapped into genuine frustrations felt by many Americans, particularly those in struggling Rust Belt communities. In interviews, JD acknowledged that Trump's appeal to working-class voters stemmed from the same anxieties and grievances he had explored in his own memoir. However, he worried that Trump's solutions were often superficial or counterproductive.

JD's decision to vote for independent candidate Evan McMullin instead of Trump further cemented his stance. For JD, this was a matter of principle. He wanted to align himself with a vision of conservatism that he believed was forward-thinking and inclusive, rather than reactionary.

These views, while reflective of JD's independent streak, also set the stage for the challenges he would face as a prospective Republican candidate in a party reshaped by Trump. His critiques became a focal point of attacks from opponents during his eventual Senate campaign, but they also underscored his willingness to speak his mind, even when it wasn't politically expedient.

CHAPTER 27

JD Vance's Journey to Catholicism: A Philosophical and Personal Transformation

In August 2019, JD took a significant step in his personal and spiritual life by being baptized into the Catholic Church. This conversion marked a profound moment for someone whose early life was shaped by the chaotic, often irreligious culture of Appalachia. For JD, the decision was deeply personal but also influenced by his intellectual encounters with the work of French philosopher René Girard, whose ideas he discovered through his friendship with Peter Thiel.

René Girard's theory of "mimetic desire" became a cornerstone of JD's spiritual transformation. According to Girard, human beings are inherently imitative in their desires, often wanting things not because of their inherent value but because others want them. This cycle of imitation fosters rivalry and, eventually, conflict. Girard's insight extends further, positing that societies historically resolve these tensions by "scapegoating" a common enemy—an individual or group upon whom they project their collective frustrations. Girard's writings interpret the life and death of Christ as a unique interruption of this cycle. Unlike previous scapegoats, Jesus is innocent and willingly sacrifices Himself, exposing humanity's destructive tendencies and offering a path toward redemption and reconciliation.

This perspective resonated deeply with JD, especially as he reflected on his own upbringing and the tribalism he saw in modern society. He recognized how mimetic desire played a role in the rivalries and conflicts of his personal life, as well as in the larger struggles of his working-class community. Girard's analysis of scapegoating also provided JD with a lens to understand the cycles of blame and resentment that often defined his social and political environment.

JD's conversion to Catholicism was not merely an intellectual exercise but a way to seek a sense of purpose and connection that transcended his individual achievements. It also reflected his growing belief in the transformative power of faith as a means of confronting and breaking free from cycles of conflict and despair.

In embracing Catholicism, JD found a worldview that aligned with his evolving values—a philosophy that acknowledged human flaws while offering hope for redemption. His journey was not just about finding faith but also about integrating his intellectual pursuits with the spiritual longing for meaning and reconciliation in a fragmented world.

The Netflix Adaptation of *Hillbilly Elegy:* A Turning Point for JD

In November 2020, Netflix released a film adaptation of JD Vance's bestselling memoir *Hillbilly Elegy*. Directed by Ron Howard and starring Gabriel Basso as JD, Glenn Close as Mamaw, and Amy Adams as Bev, the film was met with sharp criticism. While many anticipated the movie would further cement JD's voice as a bridge between Appalachia and the elite professional class, it instead became a lightning rod for controversy. The *New Yorker* dismissed the film as "a libertarian's fantasy," and other critics lambasted it for oversimplifying poverty and addiction.

For JD, the backlash to the film marked a decisive moment in his estrangement from what he referred to as "elite liberal society." Friends later described the overwhelmingly negative reception as the "last straw" in his relationship with the cultural elite. Where his book had once sparked thoughtful debate, the film became a symbol of polarization, further complicating JD's role as an interpreter of Appalachia for the mainstream.

JD saw the criticism as indicative of deeper societal issues. While some accused him of betraying his working-class roots, he felt that elite institutions were increasingly hostile to perspectives that diverged from their narratives. "Anybody who departs from the standard neoliberal orthodoxy ends up getting blasted, either from the right or the left," JD said, reflecting on the broader cultural dynamics at play.

He contrasted the reception of his memoir when it first came out with the climate after Donald Trump's election. Initially, figures like Ezra Klein and David Brooks, whom JD described as "establishmentarians," praised the book for its honest portrayal of Appalachian struggles. But after Trump's victory, JD noticed a shift. "They retreated to their tribe," he said, suggesting that once-neutral commentators became more entrenched in their ideological camps. "The institutions that enforce conventional wisdom are incredibly hostile right now."

For JD, the backlash wasn't just about the film—it reflected a broader alienation he felt from the professional class he had joined.

It underscored his belief that elite opinion-makers were unwilling to engage with narratives that challenged their worldview.

Alienation Fuels Advocacy

The criticism of the film coincided with a shift in JD's public rhetoric. While *Hillbilly Elegy* delved into what he called the "learned helplessness" of Scotch-Irish hillbilly culture, his Senate campaign and public appearances began to focus more on external factors affecting the working class. When asked about this evolution, JD pushed back on the idea that it represented a contradiction. "It made sense to talk about one thing in a memoir and the other in a Senate race," he explained.

JD argued that these narratives were interconnected rather than opposing. He highlighted the relationship between "trade and industrial policy and fatherlessness," suggesting that "we should understand deindustrialization as, in part, something that decimates working-class families, and, of course, when you destroy working-class families, then a whole lot of social pathologies move in." His remarks reflected a broader understanding of how economic and cultural forces intertwine to shape the lives of the people he grew up with.

For JD, the Netflix adaptation became more than just a failed movie—it was a turning point in his life and career. Once celebrated as a voice for the white working class, he now saw himself as an outsider to the professional class that had initially embraced him. "The institutions that enforce conventional wisdom are incredibly hostile right now," he remarked, emphasizing his disillusionment with elite cultural spaces.

Yet, this alienation seemed to strengthen JD's resolve to confront systemic challenges like deindustrialization and the opioid epidemic. Rather than focusing solely on the cultural pathologies he described in his memoir, JD shifted his attention to the broader forces—political, economic, and social—that perpetuate those struggles.

The Netflix adaptation may not have won over critics, but it served as a catalyst for JD to redefine his mission. Moving beyond the personal reflections of his memoir, he embraced a new role: one of challenging the systemic forces that keep communities like his own trapped in cycles of despair. Even as the professional class distanced itself from him, JD leaned into his identity as a conservative champion of the dispossessed. His story, once primarily about Appalachia, became a broader critique of the institutions and ideologies shaping modern America.

CHAPTER 28

The Start of His Senate Campaign

When JD announced his candidacy for the U.S. Senate in July 2021, it marked a bold new chapter in his life—one that would bridge his origins in Middletown, Ohio, with his evolution as a venture capitalist and cultural commentator. Standing before a hometown crowd, JD officially entered the race to replace retiring GOP Senator Rob Portman. It was a crowded field, but JD's unique blend of Appalachian authenticity and Silicon Valley polish made his candidacy stand out.

For JD, the decision to run wasn't just about politics—it was deeply personal. "I think we need people in Washington who are fighters—and not just fighters, but smart fighters," he told the crowd at his campaign kickoff rally. "There are a lot of fighters in Washington, D.C. They just fight for the wrong things." His words underscored the theme of his campaign: a promise to take on the entrenched political and cultural systems that he believed had failed working-class Americans, the very people he wrote about in *Hillbilly Elegy*.

Entering a Crowded and Competitive Race

JD's entry into the Republican primary added fuel to an already heated race. Other contenders included former state treasurer Josh Mandel, ex-state GOP chair Jane Timken, and businessmen Mike Gibbons and Bernie Moreno. Each candidate brought their own strengths, whether it was name recognition, early fundraising success, or ties to former President Donald Trump. Despite their efforts, no clear frontrunner had emerged, and one strategist described the race as "anybody's game."

Unlike his opponents, JD brought a unique asset: a nationally recognized name, thanks to his bestselling memoir and its Netflix adaptation. His frequent appearances on Fox News also bolstered his credibility with the GOP base. But these advantages came with challenges. His past criticisms of Trump in 2016, including a since-deleted tweet supporting independent candidate Evan McMullin, became fodder for his rivals. "Not only do we welcome him to the race, we welcome him to the Republican Party," quipped a senior adviser to Gibbons.

A Campaign Backed by Big Support

JD's Senate run wasn't just a grassroots effort; it was bolstered by significant financial backing. Peter Thiel, JD's mentor and former boss, donated $10 million to a super PAC supporting his candidacy. This early support enabled JD to launch a robust digital ad campaign, introducing his message to voters across Ohio. While his rivals leaned heavily on personal fortunes or established political connections, JD's alliance with Thiel highlighted his ability to bridge the worlds of politics, finance, and technology.

In his campaign speeches, JD leaned into themes familiar to readers of *Hillbilly Elegy*. He spoke about the struggles of working-class families, deindustrialization, and the opioid crisis—issues that had defined his childhood and shaped his worldview. But he also tackled contemporary conservative concerns, railing against critical race theory and the Biden administration's border policies. "The Senate needs someone who knows how the system works, who knows how to reform that system, and who can make this country better," JD declared.

Reconciling Past Criticisms of Trump

JD's Senate run also required him to address his complicated history with Trump. While he had criticized the former president in 2016, including a remark about Trump's rhetoric being "not in the best interest of the party or country," JD had since shifted his stance. Meeting with Trump earlier in 2021, JD sought to mend fences, framing his candidacy as part of a broader "America First" movement. For some Ohio voters, his pivot was a testament to his adaptability; for others, it raised questions about his authenticity.

Rivals like Timken and Gibbons seized on his earlier comments, positioning themselves as the true torchbearers of Trump's agenda. Timken's spokesperson called her "the only true America First candidate," while Gibbons highlighted his role as a co-chair for Trump's Ohio campaign. But JD pushed back, emphasizing his focus on the issues that mattered most to Ohioans. "Trade and industrial policy and fatherlessness," he said in one interview, "are deeply connected. When you destroy working-class families, a whole lot of social pathologies move in."

A Voice for the Dispossessed

JD's campaign aimed to channel the frustrations of the working class into political action. He presented himself as an outsider, unafraid to challenge both establishment Republicans and liberal elites. Reflecting on the cultural shifts since *Hillbilly Elegy* was published, JD remarked, "The institutions that enforce conventional wisdom are incredibly hostile right now." His candidacy, he argued, wasn't about conforming to the norms of Washington but about fighting for the people who had been left behind.

As the race intensified, JD leaned on his story—the son of a struggling single mother who defied the odds to graduate from Yale Law School and become a bestselling author. His message resonated with voters who saw their own struggles reflected in his journey. For JD, the Senate race wasn't just a political contest; it was a continuation of his lifelong mission to bridge the divide between Appalachia and the halls of power. And for the people of Ohio, it was an opportunity to decide whether JD's vision of smart, principled leadership was the kind of fight they wanted in Washington.

JD Vance's Senate Bid: A Journey Through Contradictions and Endorsements

JD Vance's decision to enter the political arena wasn't without challenges, but it was also not without drama. As a bestselling author, venture capitalist, and political newcomer, JD faced immense scrutiny as he launched his campaign for the U.S. Senate in Ohio. His candidacy stirred controversy, especially regarding his shifting relationship with Donald Trump and the GOP base he sought to court.

When JD announced his Senate run in 2021, his past comments about Trump quickly resurfaced. In 2016, during Trump's first presidential campaign, JD was openly critical. He had described himself as a "Never Trump guy," called Trump an "idiot" and "offensive," and even declared his support for independent candidate Evan McMullin. "I regret being wrong about the guy," JD admitted in a Fox News interview during his campaign, adding, "I think he was a good president. He made a lot of good decisions for people, and I think he took a lot of flak."

This public about-face became a focal point of criticism. Rivals like Josh Mandel and Mike Gibbons pounced, accusing JD of hypocrisy. The anti-tax Club for Growth aired ads reminding voters of his previous statements, branding him an opportunist. A *Daily Beast* article harshly referred to JD as a "Hypocrite's Elegy," underscoring the political tightrope he was walking. But JD leaned into his transformation, framing it as a reflection of his ability to grow and learn. "I ask folks not to judge me based on what I said in 2016," he told Fox News, "but whether I'm willing to stand up and take the heat for defending the interests of the American people."

The stakes were high in the crowded Ohio GOP primary. Competing against seasoned politicians like Mandel, former state GOP Chair Jane Timken, and businessmen Mike Gibbons and Bernie Moreno, JD sought to distinguish himself as a "smart fighter." His campaign drew on themes from *Hillbilly Elegy*, highlighting his Appalachian roots and struggles. "I think we need people in Washington who are fighters," he said at his campaign launch. "Not just fighters, but smart fighters."

JD's candidacy took a dramatic turn in April 2022 when Trump endorsed him. Trump's support came after months of deliberation and a fierce competition among candidates to secure his favor. The former president, swayed by JD's media presence and his policy positions, decided to back him despite JD's prior criticisms. "Like some others, JDmay have said some not so great things about me in the past," Trump acknowledged in his endorsement. "But he gets it now, and I have seen that in spades."

For JD, the endorsement was a game-changer. Trump's popularity among Ohio Republicans provided a significant boost, even as critics questioned the authenticity of his pivot. Trump's confidence in JD's ability to defeat the Democratic frontrunner, Tim Ryan, cemented his position as a leading candidate. "I think JD is the most likely to take out the weak, but dangerous, Democrat opponent," Trump said.

Despite the challenges, JD's campaign was emblematic of his ability to navigate complex personal and political landscapes. His journey from Trump skeptic to endorsed candidate underscored not only his adaptability but also his willingness to embrace controversy. Whether addressing his past comments or building a new political identity, JD's Senate bid became a reflection of his broader narrative—one of transformation, resilience, and a calculated readiness to fight for what he believed in.

Key Allies in JD Vance's Senate Campaign

JD Vance's rise as a candidate in Ohio's Republican Senate primary was bolstered by a trio of influential allies: Donald Trump Jr., Tucker Carlson, and Peter Thiel. Each played a pivotal role in propelling his campaign forward, providing support that combined political clout, media influence, and substantial financial backing.

Donald Trump Jr., an outspoken figure within conservative politics, became JD's primary advocate in Trump's inner circle. Known for his fiery rhetoric and strong ties to the MAGA base, Trump Jr. actively promoted JD as the candidate who could most effectively carry forward his father's agenda. His endorsement gave JD credibility among Trump's core supporters, softening the blow of JD's prior criticisms of the former president during the 2016 election. Trump Jr.'s lobbying efforts were instrumental in securing Donald Trump Sr.'s endorsement, a pivotal moment that reshaped the trajectory of JD's campaign.

In the conservative media sphere, Tucker Carlson emerged as JD's most prominent advocate. Carlson, the highest-rated cable news host, frequently praised JD on his Fox News show, showcasing his platform and helping him connect with a nationwide audience of conservative voters. Carlson's endorsement gave JD visibility and legitimacy, framing him as a champion of working-class values and a vocal critic of elites.

Meanwhile, Silicon Valley venture capitalist Peter Thiel became JD's financial anchor. Thiel, who had mentored JD during his time in Silicon Valley, invested $10 million into a super PAC supporting JD's campaign. This financial injection allowed JD to compete in a crowded primary field against well-funded opponents like Josh Mandel and Mike Gibbons. Thiel's backing also symbolized an alignment with anti-establishment, pro-tech innovation conservative ideals.

Together, these three key supporters shaped JD's campaign, bridging gaps between traditional GOP voters, Trump loyalists, and influential conservative media audiences.

CHAPTER 29

JD Vance's Immigration Agenda:
Border Walls, Cartels, and Welfare Restrictions

In his Senate campaign, JD built much of his platform on immigration and border policies, often using them as a lens to critique broader political priorities. His first campaign ad was unambiguous in its tone, as he directly asked viewers, "Are you a racist? Do you hate Mexicans?" From this provocative opening, JD sought to position himself as a champion of tough immigration measures, a stance that resonated with many Republican primary voters.

Central to JD's immigration policy was the completion of the U.S.-Mexico border wall. He repeatedly framed the border as a key issue, tying it to drug trafficking and national security concerns. During debates, he contrasted the unwillingness of Congress to fund a $4 billion border wall under Trump with the rapid approval of $14 billion for Ukraine aid under Biden. "It's a disgrace," JD argued. "We're ignoring the crisis at our own border while throwing billions at conflicts overseas."

Although JD's border wall proposal aligned with Republican orthodoxy, critics questioned its effectiveness. Research, including a Migration Policy Institute analysis, suggested that border walls often fail to halt immigration or drug trafficking, as smugglers adapt by using legal ports of entry or underground tunnels. JD dismissed such criticisms, maintaining that a strong physical barrier was an essential first step.

JD also proposed designating Mexican drug cartels as terrorist organizations. This, he argued, would provide legal and military tools to combat the cartels, including the possibility of deploying U.S. troops to Mexico. "The cartels are killing our people," he declared during a debate. "We need to treat them as the terrorists they are."

While his rhetoric appealed to many Republican voters, experts were skeptical. Vanda Felbab-Brown of the Brookings Institution noted that previous administrations had rejected such designations as impractical. "This approach adds little in terms of new tools," she said, "but it risks destabilizing U.S.-Mexico relations." Felbab-Brown also highlighted the challenges of military intervention, pointing to the U.S.'s limited success in counternarcotics operations in Afghanistan.

Welfare Restrictions for Undocumented Immigrants

Another pillar of JD's immigration platform was stopping federal welfare benefits for undocumented immigrants. He argued that the prospect of such benefits acted as a "magnet," encouraging illegal immigration. However, immigration experts countered that most federal welfare programs are already inaccessible to undocumented immigrants. Laurence Benenson of the National Immigration Forum emphasized that even lawful permanent residents face a five-year waiting period for most benefits.

JD also took issue with "mixed-status" families, where U.S.-born children of undocumented parents can qualify for certain benefits. He framed this as a loophole, though such benefits are prorated based on family composition. Critics pointed out that denying benefits to U.S.-born citizens would likely violate constitutional protections under the 14th Amendment.

In debates, JD argued that addressing border security and immigration was not just about enforcement but also about building a broader Republican coalition. He pointed to Trump's success in attracting Latino voters as evidence that strict immigration policies could coexist with economic messaging to win over minority communities.

"Woke" Questionnaires

As a senator, JD has made waves with his unconventional approach to vetting State Department nominees. His office sent questionnaires designed to uncover whether candidates for ambassadorships and other key roles were influenced by "radical" or "woke" ideologies. This initiative was part of JD's broader critique of cultural progressivism in foreign policy.

JD's concern stemmed from what he saw as U.S. diplomats imposing culturally progressive values, particularly regarding gender and LGBTQ rights, on foreign nations. He pointed to Stephanie Sullivan, a nominee for the African Union, as an example. Sullivan, who previously served as ambassador to Ghana, had advocated for LGBTQ rights in a country with conservative social norms. On the Senate floor, JD called such advocacy "cultural imperialism" and questioned its impact on U.S. national security.

"Why do we have a liberal white woman going to Africa and telling them they're not civilized enough when it comes to transgender ideology?" he asked, framing his critique as a defense of diplomatic pragmatism over cultural imposition.

While JD's questionnaires were unorthodox, he defended them as a legitimate exercise of the Senate's "advice and consent" role. He argued that career diplomats should reflect mainstream American values rather than personal ideologies. Critics, however, viewed the questionnaires as partisan overreach. Secretary of State Antony Blinken publicly criticized delays in confirming nominees, attributing them in part to JD's holds. The resulting vacancies, Blinken warned, were "undermining our national security."

Despite the backlash, JD maintained his stance, stating, "It's not extreme to ask whether someone's personal politics might compromise their ability to represent the United States effectively."

Holding CEOs Accountable for Bank Failures

In the legislative realm, JD has also shown a willingness to work across the aisle. He cosponsored a bipartisan bill aimed at holding CEOs accountable for banking failures, a move that showcased his populist leanings.

The proposed legislation sought to impose stricter penalties on executives of failed banks, including financial clawbacks and potential bans from future executive roles. JD argued that current regulations allowed CEOs to escape responsibility while taxpayers often bore the burden of bailouts.

"Too often, these executives walk away with millions while ordinary Americans suffer the consequences of their failures," JD said. "This bill is about fairness and accountability."

The bill garnered support from both sides of the aisle, reflecting growing frustration with corporate excesses. For JD, it was a chance to demonstrate that his commitment to working-class Americans extended beyond rhetoric. While his positions on immigration and culture wars often drew headlines, this legislative effort highlighted his focus on economic justice.

By blending fiery partisanship with moments of pragmatic policymaking, JD has carved out a unique space in the Senate. His approach, whether celebrated or criticized, reflects his broader effort to navigate the complexities of modern conservatism.

CHAPTER 30

Pragmatism Over Purity

JD Vance, Ohio Senate candidate and author of *Hillbilly Elegy*, found himself in a delicate political position with the CHIPS Act, a bipartisan initiative to inject nearly $300 billion into U.S. high-tech manufacturing. While the bill presented a ripe opportunity to showcase his populist America First ethos, it also challenged the balancing act JD had to maintain between his ideological commitments and practical benefits for his home state.

The CHIPS Act was a landmark piece of legislation designed to bolster semiconductor manufacturing in the U.S., reduce dependency on China, and address supply chain vulnerabilities. For Ohio, the stakes were particularly high: Intel announced plans to invest $20 billion in a semiconductor facility in the state, which would create thousands of jobs and signal a revitalization of local manufacturing.

JD's support for the bill was unequivocal in its focus on Ohio. "It is impossible for our modern economy to function without access to high-quality computer chips," he stated. "With the passage of the CHIPS Act, the Senate took an important step to ensure these products are made in America by American workers."

However, JD's endorsement of the legislation was measured and subdued. While he acknowledged the bill's economic benefits for Ohio, he tempered his support by critiquing what he called its "woke elements." His press secretary emphasized that JD would have preferred a cleaner bill, free of "Democrats' woke activism," but concluded that the potential to create critical manufacturing jobs in Ohio outweighed the legislation's flaws.

Unlike his usual populist rhetoric, JD's endorsement lacked fanfare. The campaign's official Twitter account, which has a modest following, shared a statement about the bill, while his personal account, with over 260,000 followers, remained silent. This cautious approach likely reflected the complexities of the political landscape surrounding the CHIPS Act.

JD's position on the CHIPS Act revealed the tensions inherent in his Senate campaign. While MAGA stalwarts like Marjorie Taylor Greene lambasted the legislation as "America LAST!" and criticized it as crony capitalism, other influential figures in Trump's orbit, including former National Security Adviser Robert O'Brien and U.S. Trade Representative Robert Lighthizer, endorsed it. These establishment voices underscored the national security implications of reducing dependency on Chinese semiconductors.

JD, who built his political identity on criticizing "woke capital" and foreign reliance, was forced to reconcile these broader MAGA criticisms with the practical needs of Ohio. As his opponent, Tim Ryan, pointed out, JD's support aligned with Ryan's role as a lead sponsor of the legislation. Ryan capitalized on this alignment, highlighting the CHIPS Act as a "once-in-a-lifetime opportunity" for Ohio and tying it directly to his campaign's populist, anti-China message.

Critics noted the contradictions in JD's position. David Cohen, a political science professor at the University of Akron, observed, "He's trying to sound like Jim Jordan on the campaign trail, but he's backed by big corporations and venture capitalists. It's a weird campaign."

The CHIPS Act saga illustrated the evolving political education of JD Vance. While he began his campaign as a fiery, populist outsider, this episode forced him to engage with the practical compromises of governance. Supporting the CHIPS Act, despite its alignment with a Democratic administration and criticisms from MAGA purists, demonstrated JD's willingness to prioritize tangible benefits for his constituents.

Yet, the move also exposed the challenges of his balancing act. Critics on the left and right questioned whether JD's pragmatism diluted his populist credentials. However, his supporters argued that his nuanced stance reflected a candidate focused on results rather than ideological purity.

As Ohio's Senate race tightened, with polls showing a virtual tie between JD and Ryan, the CHIPS Act became a microcosm of the broader dynamics at play in the campaign. JD's calculated support for the bill underscored his attempt to navigate the complexities of modern conservatism. He had mastered the art of threading the needle between ideology and the realities of representing a state with much at stake.

A Champion for Accountability

When a Norfolk Southern train carrying hazardous materials derailed in East Palestine, Ohio, in February 2023, it triggered not just an environmental crisis but a political one. JD Vance, a native of Middletown, Ohio, and then a freshman senator, quickly emerged as a leading voice for the affected community, balancing advocacy, criticism, and legislative action.

Less than two weeks after the derailment, JD visited East Palestine, a small village grappling with the aftermath of chemicals spilling onto land and into waterways. He posted a video walking along a creek, showing visible chemicals contaminating the water. "The fact that these chemicals are still seeping into the ground is an insult to the people who live in East Palestine," he said, highlighting the dire need for immediate action.

JD called on President Biden to stop blaming former President Donald Trump for the derailment and focus on solutions. "Stop blaming Donald Trump, a guy who hasn't been president for three years, and use the powers of the federal government to help the people in this community," JD told Fox News. His rhetoric underscored the frustration of East Palestine residents, who felt abandoned by federal agencies.

JD's advocacy drew national attention, especially when he joined Donald Trump during a visit to East Palestine on February 22, 2023. Trump, alongside JD and other Ohio lawmakers, distributed water, food, and supplies to residents in need. The visit contrasted with President Biden's absence, a point JD hammered home, stating, "Donald Trump showed up in East Palestine, and Joe Biden never did."

The Railway Safety Act

As the immediate crisis evolved into a broader debate about railway safety, JD pivoted to legislative action. Alongside fellow Ohio Senator Sherrod Brown, a Democrat, JD introduced the Railway Safety Act of 2023. The bipartisan measure sought to impose stricter safety standards on rail companies, including heightened requirements for hazardous material transport and expanded emergency response measures.

The bill initially gained significant momentum, supported by Democrats and a handful of Republicans. However, it stalled in Congress, with Senate Majority Leader Chuck Schumer hesitant to bring it to a vote without securing enough Republican support to bypass a filibuster. JD voiced his frustration, saying, "It makes no sense that we could be a year out and still have Congress sitting on its hands."

Despite the legislative gridlock, JD remained optimistic. He claimed to have private assurances from Republican colleagues that they would support the bill. "I think we'll get more than 60 votes on the Railway Safety bill, but it does require Schumer to bring it to the floor," he stated. JD emphasized the need for urgency, calling it "absurd" that the Senate couldn't allocate two days of floor time to pass the bill.

JD didn't shy away from criticizing both the Biden administration and Norfolk Southern. He argued that residents felt "abandoned" by the federal government and accused Norfolk Southern of failing to take sufficient responsibility. "People need long-term health monitoring, and the company should pay for it," he said, echoing community concerns about lingering health risks and environmental damage.

Transportation Secretary Pete Buttigieg also drew JD's ire. Buttigieg, acknowledging the delay in passing the Railway Safety Act, said it was "frustrating" that Congress had not acted decisively. JD responded by emphasizing the need for immediate action rather than platitudes, stating that federal agencies must prioritize East Palestine's recovery.

Nearly a year after the derailment, East Palestine residents like Bonnie Davis voiced ongoing concerns about their health and the possibility of another disaster. "We've heard of derailments in other little places," Davis said, expressing the widespread anxiety among small communities reliant on rail transport.

JD revisited East Palestine in early 2024, reaffirming his commitment to the community. His efforts kept the spotlight on the village long after the national media's attention waned. "We can't forget East Palestine," JD emphasized, arguing that federal agencies and Norfolk Southern must remain accountable for long-term environmental testing and healthcare for residents.

Sherrod Brown, co-sponsor of the Railway Safety Act, praised JD's commitment but urged the Biden administration to listen to residents. "The president needs to hear from people about what's happening and ensure everything is back to normal," Brown said. JD echoed this sentiment, underscoring the importance of community voices in shaping policy responses.

Political Implications

JD's advocacy during the East Palestine crisis cemented his reputation as a populist champion willing to challenge federal agencies and corporations alike. His quick response and visible presence earned him national attention, while his legislative push showcased his ability to work across the aisle. However, the stalled progress of the Railway Safety Act highlighted the challenges of navigating a deeply divided Congress.

Critics questioned whether JD's alignment with Trump might limit his bipartisan appeal, while supporters praised his unflinching defense of Ohio's working-class communities. For JD, the crisis underscored his core message: the federal government and corporate elites often fail to prioritize ordinary Americans.

As President Biden prepared to visit East Palestine over a year after the derailment, JD reiterated his demands for accountability. "This visit shouldn't just be a photo op," JD said. "The president needs to commit to long-term solutions for the people of East Palestine."

The East Palestine train derailment became a defining moment for JD Vance's early Senate career. His hands-on approach, from wading into contaminated creeks to drafting bipartisan legislation, reflected his commitment to the people of Ohio. The Railway Safety Act, even in limbo, symbolized his broader fight against corporate negligence and government inaction.

While East Palestine's recovery remains incomplete, JD's efforts have ensured that the crisis—and the community's needs—are not forgotten. For JD Vance, the derailment wasn't just a political challenge but a personal mission to advocate for the overlooked and underserved.

CHAPTER 31

JD Vance's Stance on Ukraine in 2022:
A Focus on Domestic Priorities

In 2022, JD emerged as a prominent voice questioning U.S. support for Ukraine, framing his critique through a lens of prioritizing American interests. His controversial remark on Steve Bannon's podcast—"I got to be honest with you, I don't really care what happens to Ukraine one way or another"—captured the essence of his position and sparked widespread debate. JD's perspective was rooted in his belief that American resources and attention were being misallocated to foreign conflicts at the expense of pressing domestic issues.

JD expressed deep skepticism about the bipartisan support for U.S. involvement in Ukraine amid Russia's invasion. While many politicians framed the conflict as a critical test of democracy versus autocracy, JD questioned whether such framing justified the significant financial and military aid being sent overseas. His criticism stemmed from a conviction that these resources could be better spent addressing crises closer to home, such as border security, the opioid epidemic, and the struggles of working-class Americans.

JD viewed the Ukraine war as emblematic of what he saw as a misguided foreign policy establishment in Washington, D.C. He argued that the United States was repeating the mistakes of the Iraq and Afghanistan wars by prioritizing interventionism over the needs of its own citizens. "We've spent decades fighting endless wars overseas, wasting trillions of dollars, and what do we have to show for it?" JD asked in interviews and speeches. To him, the bipartisan consensus on Ukraine reflected the same pattern of prioritizing elite interests and global ambitions over the well-being of ordinary Americans.

JD frequently linked his stance on Ukraine to broader concerns about the U.S. economy. He argued that the billions of dollars allocated to Ukraine could instead be used to rebuild American infrastructure, fund healthcare initiatives, or combat the fentanyl crisis that has devastated communities like his own in Ohio. "We can't afford to be the world's policeman when our own country is falling apart," he said, calling for a reorientation of federal spending toward domestic priorities.

Despite his skepticism, JD's position did not mean he was entirely dismissive of Ukraine's plight. He acknowledged the tragedy of the conflict but maintained that the responsibility for aiding Ukraine should fall primarily on European nations. JD criticized what he saw as a lack of proportional contributions from Europe compared to the United States. "Why are we footing the bill while Germany and France stand on the sidelines?" he asked, challenging the notion that the U.S. should bear the brunt of the financial and military burden.

Ultimately, JD's stance on Ukraine in 2022 reflected his broader political philosophy: a commitment to prioritizing American citizens and questioning the priorities of the political elite. While his remarks generated controversy, they resonated with voters who shared his concerns about the impact of U.S. foreign policy on domestic issues, reinforcing his position as a populist voice challenging the Washington consensus.

Allegations Against the Biden Administration

JD has been one of the most vocal critics of the Biden administration's handling of the fentanyl crisis, linking the issue directly to policies at the southern border. In a stark and controversial statement, JD suggested that the administration's failure to curb the flow of fentanyl into the United States might be intentional, accusing President Biden of targeting Republican-leaning regions. "If you wanted to kill a bunch of MAGA voters in the middle of the heartland, how better than to target them and their kids with this deadly fentanyl. . . . It does look intentional. It's like Joe Biden wants to punish the people who didn't vote for him," JD declared, underscoring his view that the administration's inaction is not merely neglect but potentially calculated.

Fentanyl, a synthetic opioid significantly more potent than morphine, has wreaked havoc on communities across America, particularly in working-class and rural regions. For JD, the issue is deeply personal, reflecting his upbringing in Ohio, where the opioid epidemic has devastated families and communities. He sees the fentanyl crisis as a direct consequence of what he calls an "open border policy" that allows drug cartels to operate with impunity. According to JD, the Biden administration's approach has emboldened these cartels, increasing the supply of fentanyl and exacerbating the national epidemic.

JD's assertion that the crisis may be intentional is grounded in his broader critique of political elites. He frequently argues that Washington, D.C., prioritizes globalist agendas over the well-being of average Americans. By framing the fentanyl crisis as a political weapon, JD connects it to a larger narrative of neglect and animosity toward Trump voters. His comments resonate with many conservatives who see the crisis not just as a public health failure but as a symptom of deeper political divides.

However, his remarks have sparked significant backlash, with critics accusing him of spreading conspiracy theories and stoking partisan tensions. Despite the controversy, JD remains steadfast, calling for stricter border policies, harsher penalties for traffickers, and a comprehensive crackdown on fentanyl production and distribution.

The Immigration Debate

JD Vance's critique of immigration policy, especially under the Biden administration, reflects his broader commitment to an America First agenda. Central to his argument is the idea that lax border policies have facilitated the rise of crises, including drug trafficking, economic displacement, and cultural fragmentation. Immigration has become a cornerstone of JD's platform, particularly as it relates to the southern border and its impact on working-class Americans.

Republicans, including JD, typically frame immigration as a national security and economic issue. They argue that an unchecked border fuels drug trafficking, as seen with the fentanyl crisis, and undermines American wages by introducing low-cost labor. JD has explicitly connected these issues, contending that "illegal immigration depresses wages for American workers and drives a wedge between communities." He has championed policies such as completing the border wall, increasing funding for border enforcement, and implementing stricter penalties for illegal crossings. His rhetoric often emphasizes the need to prioritize American citizens over undocumented immigrants.

On the other hand, Democrats tend to approach immigration from a humanitarian perspective, advocating for comprehensive reform that addresses the needs of both immigrants and the broader society. They argue for pathways to citizenship, protections for DACA recipients, and better management of asylum processes. The Biden administration's stance has focused on balancing enforcement with compassion, but critics like JD argue that this approach has failed, creating what he describes as an "open border" that exacerbates drug trafficking and human smuggling.

The partisan divide is stark. While Democrats highlight the economic and cultural contributions of immigrants, Republicans, including JD, emphasize the strain on public resources and the perceived threat to national identity. JD frequently critiques what he sees as Democratic hypocrisy, accusing the left of supporting policies that harm the very communities they claim to champion.

For JD, immigration is not just a policy issue but a cultural battleground. He frames it as a struggle between globalist elites and everyday Americans, arguing that the current system serves corporate interests at the expense of working families. By tying immigration to broader issues like crime, wages, and the fentanyl crisis, JD underscores his belief that comprehensive border security is essential to preserving America's future. His stance resonates with many voters who feel left behind by rapid demographic and economic changes, reinforcing his position as a leading voice in the contemporary immigration debate.

Trump Indictments

In June 2023, JD took a bold stand against the Biden administration. He placed a hold on all Justice Department appointments. This move was a direct response to the indictments of former President Donald Trump. JD believed the charges were politically motivated. He argued that the Justice Department was being weaponized against Trump and his supporters.

JD did not shy away from defending Trump publicly. He called the hush-money trial in New York a "threat to American democracy." For JD, this case represented more than legal charges. It symbolized a deeper problem: the use of political power to silence opponents. He frequently voiced concerns that such actions eroded trust in the justice system.

This stance put JD at the forefront of Trump's defenders in the Senate. Many Republicans praised him for standing firm. Critics, however, accused him of undermining legal institutions. JD dismissed these claims. He argued that his actions were about fairness and accountability, not partisanship.

JD's hold on appointments was a controversial move. It delayed key nominations in the Justice Department. Some saw it as a bold act of resistance, while others viewed it as obstruction. For JD, the message was clear: the government should serve the people, not target political rivals.

This episode reflected JD's broader commitment to challenging the political establishment. He often framed his actions as a defense of democracy and the rule of law. Whether one agreed with his tactics or not, JD's firm stand made him a key figure in the Republican Party's ongoing battle over Trump's legacy.

JD Vance's Culture War Initiatives in the Senate

JD believed that culture and class were deeply connected. He often said, "The culture war is class war." For him, opposing the cultural values of progressive elites was essential. He believed it was the only way to protect the economic and political interests of the working class.

In the Senate, JD focused on several cultural issues. One of his most controversial proposals was a bill criminalizing gender-affirming care for transgender minors. He argued that such treatments were harmful and unnecessary. Critics accused him of targeting vulnerable groups, but JD insisted he was protecting children from irreversible decisions.

JD also championed a ban on federal mask mandates. He saw these mandates as overreach by the government. For JD, such policies symbolized the loss of personal freedoms during the pandemic. His efforts gained support among voters who were frustrated with ongoing COVID-19 restrictions.

Another key initiative was his crackdown on affirmative action policies in colleges and universities. JD believed these policies were unfair and perpetuated division. He argued for a merit-based system that treated all students equally, regardless of their background. This stance sparked heated debates about equality and fairness.

On abortion, JD supported a 15-week ban with exceptions for rape, incest, and threats to the mother's life. He saw this as a balanced approach that respected life while acknowledging complex circumstances. His position aligned with many conservatives but also reflected some willingness to compromise.

JD's culture war initiatives reflected his broader philosophy. He believed progressive policies hurt the working class by focusing on identity politics instead of real economic issues. For JD, standing against these cultural shifts was not just about values—it was about protecting the future of American families.

CABINET

'n some ways, Trump's large, national coalition defies easy characterization. He draws from a broad base of good people: kind folks who open their homes and hearts to people of all colors and creeds, married couples with happy homes and families who live nearby, public servants who put their lives on the line to fight fires in their communities.'

CHAPTER 33

A Political Transformation

By 2016, JD was the author of *Hillbilly Elegy*, a memoir that resonated deeply with readers across the political spectrum. His book captured the struggles of the white working class and offered a lens into the social and economic disarray that fueled Donald Trump's rise to power. At the time, JD positioned himself as a critic of Trump, frequently voicing opposition to the then-presidential candidate's rhetoric and policies. Yet, by 2024, JD had transformed into a staunch Trump ally and one of the most influential voices in the MAGA movement.

JD's journey was one of gradual, personal, and political evolution, shaped by his disillusionment with the American elite and his growing recognition of Trump's role as a disruptor of the status quo. His transformation was not merely about aligning with Trump's policies but about rethinking his own place in a political system he came to view as fundamentally broken.

In the wake of *Hillbilly Elegy's* success, JD found himself in an unexpected position. His book, lauded for its compassionate and incisive portrayal of working-class struggles, had become a bestseller among educated liberals attempting to understand Trump's appeal. For many, JD was a "whisperer" for Trump's base, someone who could articulate the motivations of those who had been left behind by globalization and cultural shifts. However, JD soon grew uncomfortable with how his narrative was being co-opted.

"People were trying to understand Trump's voters without challenging their own assumptions about those people," JD reflected. Over time, he began to see his role not as a neutral explainer but as a participant in a broader cultural and political divide. This realization marked the beginning of his departure from the liberal elite circles that had embraced him.

A pivotal moment came in 2018 when JD attended a Business Roundtable dinner. Seated next to a prominent CEO, he listened as the executive lamented being forced to pay higher wages due to tightened immigration policies under Trump. The conversation struck a nerve. The CEO assumed JD would sympathize with his plight, but JD found himself siding with the workers who now had access to better-paying jobs. "That moment made me realize I was on the wrong train," JD later admitted. "I had to get off before I woke up in 10 years and hated everything I had become."

A Shift Toward Trump

JD's disillusionment with the elite extended to both sides of the political spectrum. He grew increasingly critical of the "bipartisan consensus" that had dominated American politics for decades, arguing that it had failed the working class. Trump's presidency, despite its controversies, represented a break from this consensus, particularly on issues like trade, immigration, and foreign policy.

JD came to appreciate Trump's willingness to challenge entrenched norms, even as he struggled with the stylistic elements of Trump's leadership. "Like a lot of others, I focused too much on Trump's style and not enough on his substance," JD reflected. Over time, he recognized that Trump's populist critique of the establishment aligned with his own growing frustrations.

By 2020, JD had fully embraced Trump's agenda. He voted for him in the presidential election, a decision that marked a significant departure from his earlier stance. For JD, this shift was about more than policy; it was about defending the concerns of Trump's voters, whom he felt had been dismissed and maligned by the media and political elites.

The events surrounding the 2020 election and January 6th, 2021, were pivotal in shaping JD's political outlook. While he did not condone the violence at the Capitol, he viewed the broader debate over election integrity as a symptom of deeper systemic issues. JD criticized what he saw as media suppression of key stories and last-minute changes to voting rules during the pandemic, arguing that these factors had undermined public trust in the electoral process.

"Challenging elections is part of the democratic process," JD asserted, pushing back against accusations that Trump's actions threatened democracy. At the same time, he expressed frustration with the lack of a coherent strategy from Trump's legal team, calling it a "legal clown show." Despite these critiques, JD maintained that Trump's willingness to voice the frustrations of his base was vital to addressing the systemic failures of American democracy.

A Populist Vision for America

As JD transitioned into his role as a U.S. senator, he became a leading advocate for populist economic policies. He called for higher wages for American workers, stricter immigration controls, and tariffs to incentivize domestic manufacturing. "The trade issue and the immigration issue are two sides of the same coin," JD argued, emphasizing the need to prioritize American labor over cheaper alternatives abroad.

JD also championed regulatory reforms to spur innovation in energy and infrastructure, framing these efforts as essential to rebuilding America's industrial base. His vision was rooted in the belief that economic policy should serve the interests of working-class Americans rather than corporate elites.

JD's relationship with Trump deepened on a personal level as well. He recalled an early meeting with Trump in 2021, where the former president expressed frustration over military leaders manipulating troop redeployment numbers. For JD, this interaction revealed a side of Trump that was rarely acknowledged by the media—a leader deeply concerned with exercising authority in the face of bureaucratic resistance. "He's much more complex than people give him credit for," JD noted.

Trump's support for JD during his Senate campaign further solidified their bond. "He called me out of the blue to remind me there's a lot of love out there," JD recounted, describing Trump's encouragement as a source of strength during a challenging campaign.

By 2024, JD stood as one of the most influential figures in the MAGA movement, potentially poised to serve as Trump's running mate in the upcoming election. His transformation from a critic to a staunch ally reflected both his personal evolution and the shifting dynamics of American politics.

JD framed his journey not as a betrayal of his earlier ideals but as a fulfillment of his commitment to addressing the systemic failures that had long plagued working-class Americans. As he looked to the future, JD remained steadfast in his belief that meaningful change required challenging the entrenched norms of the political and economic elite—a mission he believed Trump was uniquely equipped to lead.

CHAPTER 34

The Legacy of 2020

Donald J. Trump's rise to become the Republican presidential nominee in 2024 was a saga defined by resilience, dominance, and a calculated alignment with the shifting dynamics of his party. Defying critics, political scandals, and even legal challenges, Trump reaffirmed his grip on the Republican base, leveraging his populist rhetoric, an unshakable connection with his supporters, and an uncanny ability to capitalize on political turbulence.

The road to 2024 was paved with the embers of the 2020 election. Trump's controversial claims of a stolen election and his refusal to accept defeat left an indelible mark on American politics. While many predicted his political demise after the Capitol riots on January 6, 2021, Trump's base remained fiercely loyal. Polls in the aftermath showed his enduring popularity among Republican voters, signaling his continued relevance in the GOP.

In the two years following his presidency, Trump played the role of kingmaker in the Republican Party, endorsing candidates and rallying support for midterm elections. Even when his picks didn't always secure victories, his ability to dominate headlines and influence primary contests underscored his unrivaled position. His leadership PAC amassed an unprecedented war chest, allowing him to fund allies and maintain his political machinery.

By 2023, Trump was navigating a storm of legal challenges, from ongoing investigations into his business dealings to the classified documents case. These legal battles, rather than diminishing his appeal, galvanized his base. Trump and his allies portrayed him as a victim of political persecution, framing the legal challenges as evidence of the establishment's fear of his power. This narrative resonated deeply with his supporters, who viewed him as a fighter against a corrupt system.

His rivals in the Republican Party, including potential challengers like Florida Governor Ron DeSantis and former Vice President Mike Pence, struggled to capitalize on these scandals. Instead, Trump's ability to weather the controversies further solidified his image as a defiant outsider, unyielding in the face of adversity.

The GOP Landscape: Trump vs. the Field

The 2024 Republican primary field was initially crowded, featuring figures like DeSantis, Pence, Nikki Haley, and others aiming to present themselves as viable alternatives to Trump. However, they faced a formidable obstacle: Trump's unwavering grip on the GOP base. Polls consistently showed Trump with a commanding lead, often garnering over 50% support among Republican voters, while his closest rival trailed by double digits.

DeSantis, once considered a strong contender, failed to distinguish himself from Trump's brand of politics. His policies mirrored Trump's populism, but he lacked the charisma and unfiltered rhetoric that endeared Trump to his base. Pence's campaign leaned heavily on his role in the Trump administration, but his break with Trump over the certification of the 2020 election alienated a significant portion of the Republican electorate.

The dynamics of the GOP primary showcased the challenge of running against Trump: candidates had to appeal to his base without alienating it, a near-impossible balancing act. As a result, Trump dominated debates, rallies, and media coverage, often reducing his opponents to afterthoughts.

Campaign Strategy: Populism Reloaded

Trump's 2024 campaign was a refined version of his earlier runs. He doubled down on his America First platform, emphasizing economic nationalism, immigration restrictions, and a hardline stance on foreign policy. At campaign rallies, Trump railed against "woke" culture, the "deep state," and what he called the corrupt establishment. His speeches were laced with grievances from his presidency, but they also resonated with millions of voters who felt disillusioned with the direction of the country under Joe Biden's administration.

Trump's team employed sophisticated digital strategies to target voters. Social media platforms were flooded with campaign ads, memes, and videos, capitalizing on the loyalty of his online supporters. Trump's rallies, once again a hallmark of his campaign, drew massive crowds, reinforcing his message of being the voice of the people against the elites.

His narrative of victimhood, coupled with promises to "finish what he started" in his first term, struck a chord with voters who believed he was the only candidate capable of restoring their vision of America.

Several moments defined Trump's dominance in the primary season:

1. **Announcement in Mar-a-Lago:** In late 2022, Trump officially announced his candidacy at Mar-a-Lago. The event, though smaller than his past rallies, set the tone for his campaign. Trump promised to "restore American greatness" and reclaim the White House, portraying himself as the nation's savior.

2. **Rhetorical Attacks on Rivals:** Trump's knack for branding his opponents with derisive nicknames proved as effective as ever. He referred to DeSantis as "Ron DeSanctimonious" and mocked Pence as "Little Mike." These jabs, while ridiculed by critics, dominated media coverage and further weakened his rivals.

3. **Key Endorsements:** Trump secured endorsements from influential figures like Senator JDand House Speaker Kevin McCarthy. These endorsements signaled the party's continued alignment with Trump's vision and added credibility to his campaign.

4. **Debate Stage Presence:** Trump's dominance extended to the debate stage, where his charisma and combative style overshadowed his rivals. He effectively painted himself as the only candidate capable of taking on Biden and the Democrats.

5. **Legal Drama:** The spectacle of Trump's legal battles became a campaign tool. His arraignment in New York City, widely covered by the media, became a rallying cry for his supporters. Trump turned each court appearance into a fundraising opportunity, further energizing his base.

A Party United—Mostly

By the time Super Tuesday arrived, Trump had an insurmountable lead in delegates. His victories in key early states like Iowa, New Hampshire, and South Carolina solidified his status as the presumptive nominee. The momentum carried him through the remaining primaries, where his opponents struggled to gain traction.

While Trump faced resistance from a faction of the Republican Party, the majority of the GOP coalesced around his candidacy. Establishment figures who had once distanced themselves from Trump returned to his fold, recognizing his dominance over the party's base. Even those who had been critical of Trump in the past conceded that he was the Republican Party's best chance of retaking the White House.

As the Republican nominee, Trump entered the general election campaign with significant advantages. His fundraising machine was unparalleled, his voter base deeply loyal, and his media presence unmatched. However, he also faced formidable challenges, including opposition from Democrats galvanized by the threat of a Trump return and independents wary of his polarizing style.

Trump's return as the GOP's standard-bearer in 2024 symbolized his resilience and the enduring appeal of his brand of politics. His journey from the aftermath of the 2020 election to reclaiming the Republican nomination underscored his unique ability to dominate the political landscape, ensuring his place as one of the most influential figures in modern American history.

CHAPTER 35

A Shortlist Emerges

As the 2024 Republican National Convention approached, the race to become Donald Trump's vice-presidential running mate was a saga of political maneuvering, calculated decisions, and intense speculation. The process highlighted Trump's strategic focus on loyalty, electoral advantage, and compatibility with his own populist brand. Among the candidates considered for this coveted role, JD emerged as a prominent contender, cementing his status as a central figure in the Trump campaign.

By June 2024, Trump's campaign had narrowed the pool of potential running mates to a shortlist of nine candidates, reflecting a mix of political experience, geographic appeal, and alignment with Trump's agenda. Among those on the list were sitting senators, a governor, and high-profile Republican figures. Four candidates—Doug Burgum, Marco Rubio, Tim Scott, and JD Vance—were reportedly sent vetting materials, though Rubio publicly denied this.

The campaign also requested information from other notable names, including Ben Carson, Tom Cotton, Byron Donalds, and Elise Stefanik. Later in mid-June, Trump himself revealed that Virginia Governor Glenn Youngkin was also under consideration, signaling the fluidity of the decision-making process.

Trump's decision-making process for choosing a running mate revolved around several key criteria. First, he sought unwavering loyalty, a hallmark of his political relationships. The vice-presidential pick needed to align closely with Trump's America First agenda and demonstrate the ability to defend it vigorously.

Second, the candidate had to enhance the ticket's electoral appeal. With battleground states playing a pivotal role in the 2024 election, geographic and demographic considerations loomed large. Trump's team explored candidates who could energize Republican voters, appeal to independents, and chip away at Democratic strongholds.

Finally, compatibility with Trump's persona and style was essential. The running mate had to complement Trump's charisma, counterbalance his polarizing reputation, and bring policy expertise or electoral advantages to the table.

Finalists and Challenges

As the vetting process progressed, the field of candidates narrowed. By late June, reports indicated that the three leading contenders were Doug Burgum, Marco Rubio, and JD Vance. Each presented unique strengths and challenges.

Burgum, the governor of North Dakota, brought executive experience and a reputation for pragmatic leadership. However, his low national profile and lack of connection to Trump's core base were potential drawbacks.

Rubio, a senator from Florida and a former presidential candidate, offered extensive experience in foreign policy and strong ties to the Hispanic community. Yet, his residency in Florida complicated matters due to constitutional restrictions against a presidential and vice-presidential candidate residing in the same state.

JD Vance, the first-term senator from Ohio, stood out for his ideological alignment with Trump's populist agenda and his appeal to working-class voters in the Rust Belt. His rapid ascent in the GOP, fueled by his memoir *Hillbilly Elegy* and his vocal support for Trump, made him a compelling choice.

Tim Scott, another finalist, was a senator from South Carolina and a 2024 presidential candidate. His optimistic vision of conservatism and ability to reach diverse voter groups made him a strong contender, though his softer rhetoric contrasted with Trump's combative style.

By June 21, speculation intensified as NBC News reported that Burgum and JD had become the primary focus of Trump's deliberations, with Rubio's prospects fading due to logistical challenges. CNN added that Scott was still in contention, though his chances appeared slimmer compared to the other finalists.

Trump's campaign employed secrecy and suspense to heighten interest in the announcement. Reports suggested that the selected running mate would likely be revealed at the Republican National Convention. However, Trump remained deliberately vague, keeping the media and political observers guessing.

In late June, the campaign leaked hints about the imminent decision. On June 22, NBC News confirmed that Trump had chosen his vice-presidential pick, with the selected candidate expected to attend a debate on June 27. The Associated Press later reported that the nominee already had a dedicated plane awaiting customization with their name—a testament to the significance of the announcement.

Despite the mounting anticipation, Trump continued to keep his final choice under wraps. Jason Miller, a senior Trump adviser, stated that the announcement could come in the week leading up to the convention or even during the event itself. Trump echoed this sentiment, emphasizing the dramatic flair that had become his hallmark.

Building Momentum

The process of selecting Trump's running mate underscored the importance of the vice-presidential role in the 2024 election. The Republican ticket needed to energize the party's base, counter the Biden-Harris campaign, and navigate a polarized political landscape.

Throughout this period, JD remained a central figure in the discussions. His journey from venture capitalist and bestselling author to senator and now a potential vice-presidential nominee exemplified his rapid ascent in Republican politics. JD's close alignment with Trump's America First vision and his ability to connect with working-class voters in key states like Ohio bolstered his case.

The eventual announcement of Trump's running mate was not just a pivotal moment for the 2024 campaign—it also reflected the evolving dynamics of the Republican Party under Trump's leadership. As the convention approached, the spotlight remained firmly fixed on the candidates, with the nation awaiting Trump's decision with bated breath. The choice of running mate would not only shape the Republican ticket but also set the tone for the general election and beyond.

CHAPTER 36

Chapter: JDand the Weight of Controversy

As JDnavigated his rapid rise in politics, his statements and opinions often sparked heated debates, placing him at the center of national controversies. From his remarks on childlessness in leadership roles to criticisms of teachers without children, these episodes highlighted the polarizing nature of his rhetoric and the challenges of his populist appeal.

Controversial Remarks on Childlessness in Leadership (July 2024)

One of the most significant controversies in JD's career reignited in July 2024 when comments he made in 2021 resurfaced. During a public conversation, JD had criticized childless individuals in leadership positions, deriding them as "childless cat ladies." The statement had initially flown under the radar but reemerged during his tenure as a prominent senator and Trump's vice-presidential running mate.

JD framed his argument around the idea that leaders with children might be more invested in the long-term future of the nation. "How can people who don't have a personal stake in the future," he asked, "make the best decisions for the next generation?" While his remarks resonated with some segments of his base, who viewed it as a defense of family values, others saw it as a blatant attack on people's personal choices and circumstances.

Critics argued that JD's comments were exclusionary, stigmatizing individuals who, for various reasons, do not have children. They pointed out that his remarks perpetuated harmful stereotypes and dismissed the contributions of many childless leaders throughout history. Prominent figures, including business leaders, activists, and politicians, condemned his statement, framing it as a reflection of his broader worldview that prioritized traditional family structures over inclusivity.

In response to the backlash, JD doubled down on his position, stating in an interview, "I believe family is fundamental to our society, and leaders who understand the value of children have a unique perspective on what it means to secure a future worth fighting for." While this stance reaffirmed his commitment to family-centric policies, it further alienated detractors who accused him of being out of touch with the diverse realities of modern society.

Criticism of Teachers Without Children (August 2024)

A month after the "childless cat ladies" controversy, JD faced another firestorm when audio from 2021 surfaced, revealing his criticism of childless teachers. In the recording, JD specifically mentioned Randi Weingarten, a prominent union leader, as someone who didn't have children yet influenced policies affecting millions of students. He expressed discomfort with the idea of childless educators having significant sway over children's upbringing, stating, "If you don't have kids, how can you understand what it means to shape a young mind?"

This controversy amplified existing debates about education policy and the role of teachers in shaping society. Supporters of JD's comments argued that his remarks underscored the importance of lived experience in decision-making, especially when it comes to children. To them, his criticism was not a personal attack but a broader commentary on the disconnect between policymakers and the realities faced by parents and families.

However, the backlash was swift and widespread. Teachers' unions and education advocates lambasted his remarks, calling them demeaning and dismissive of educators' dedication and expertise. Randi Weingarten herself responded, saying, "To suggest that a teacher's worth is tied to whether or not they have children is both insulting and ignorant. Teaching is about skill, empathy, and commitment, not biology."

JD's critics accused him of perpetuating the idea that only parents are capable of understanding children's needs, a perspective they argued undermines the professionalism and hard work of countless educators. Many pointed out that some of the most beloved and effective teachers in history did not have children of their own and that parenting and teaching, while related, are distinct roles.

In response to the uproar, JD clarified his remarks, stating that his intent was to highlight the value of parental perspectives in policymaking rather than to diminish the contributions of childless teachers. He said, "My comments were aimed at ensuring that our education policies are informed by the experiences of parents. I deeply respect the work of teachers, whether they have children or not, and recognize their dedication to shaping our future."

The Impact on JD's Public Image

Both controversies painted JD as a figure unafraid to voice opinions that resonated with certain conservative values, even at the risk of alienating broader audiences. For many in his base, these statements reaffirmed his commitment to family and traditional roles, a cornerstone of his populist appeal. They viewed his remarks as a defense against what they saw as the erosion of family values and an overly bureaucratic education system.

However, to his detractors, these controversies were emblematic of a deeper issue: a perceived inability to appreciate the diverse realities of modern society. Critics saw his comments as indicative of a worldview that was rigid, exclusionary, and dismissive of people's lived experiences outside the traditional family structure.

Political analysts noted that these controversies underscored the delicate balance JD needed to maintain as a rising star in Republican politics. His appeal to working-class and religious voters hinged on his ability to champion their values unapologetically. Yet, his broader electability depended on not alienating suburban and independent voters who might view his comments as divisive.

Lessons from Controversy

The debates surrounding JD's remarks on childlessness and education policy underscored a recurring theme in his political career: his willingness to tackle contentious issues head-on, even if it meant enduring public backlash. These moments highlighted the challenges of navigating cultural debates in an era of heightened political polarization, where every statement was scrutinized and amplified.

For JD, these controversies also served as a reminder of the power and responsibility of words. While his unapologetic approach endeared him to his base, it also underscored the importance of carefully framing his arguments to avoid alienating potential supporters. As he continued his rise in politics, these episodes became part of the larger narrative of a leader unafraid to challenge societal norms, for better or worse.

In the end, these controversies, like many others in JD's career, showcased the duality of his political persona: a champion of traditional values to his supporters, and a polarizing figure to his critics. As his journey in public life continued, these debates remained central to the evolving perception of JD in the American political landscape.

CHAPTER 37

Immigration Allegations

In September 2024, JD found himself at the center of another heated controversy, this time involving incendiary allegations about Haitian immigrants in Springfield, Ohio. The claims, which included accusations of pet abductions, heightened public tensions and drew sharp criticism, while also revealing JD's unapologetically combative approach to addressing immigration issues.

The controversy began when JD alleged that Haitian immigrants in Springfield were "draining social services and generally causing chaos." His claims escalated when he further asserted that there were reports of immigrants abducting and eating pets, particularly cats. "Reports now show that people have had their pets abducted and eaten by people who shouldn't be in this country," JD stated publicly. His remarks quickly gained traction within conservative circles, with former President Donald Trump echoing the allegations during a presidential debate.

Springfield authorities, however, immediately refuted the claims. The local government issued a statement saying there were "no credible reports or specific claims" of such incidents and emphasized that the Haitian immigrants in the area were present legally. Nonetheless, JD doubled down on his rhetoric, urging his supporters to continue sharing memes about the alleged pet abductions. "Keep the cat memes flowing," he told his followers, blending humor with his political messaging.

Adding fuel to the fire, JD promoted an unverified allegation by conservative activist Christopher Rufo, who claimed that African migrants in Dayton, Ohio, were engaging in similar behavior. Dayton authorities, like their counterparts in Springfield, categorically denied the claims, stating that there was "no evidence to even remotely suggest that any group, including our immigrant community, is engaged in eating pets."

Even as the allegations were widely disputed, JD pivoted to another narrative, claiming that a child in Springfield had been murdered by a Haitian migrant. The statement quickly unraveled when local reports clarified that the child had tragically died in a vehicular accident, not as a result of any criminal act by an immigrant. The father of the deceased child publicly condemned JD for exploiting his child's death for political gain, calling the remarks "disrespectful and hurtful."

Public Backlash and Bomb Threats

The controversy didn't stop at the disputed claims. JD went on to allege that Springfield was experiencing a "massive rise in communicable diseases" due to the presence of Haitian migrants. Once again, local authorities, including the Clark County health commissioner, debunked the claims, reporting no substantial increase in communicable diseases in the area.

As the allegations and rhetoric continued to spread, the situation in Springfield became increasingly volatile. The city experienced multiple bomb threats in September 2024, creating a climate of fear and instability. Though JD publicly denounced the threats, stating, "I oppose violence or the threat of violence levied against Springfield," he did not back down from his allegations. Critics accused him of fueling the tensions that led to these threats through his inflammatory rhetoric.

In a particularly controversial moment, JD admitted to his supporters that his claims about immigrants eating pets might not be accurate. "It's possible, of course, that all of these rumors will turn out to be false," he said. However, he defended his actions by arguing that his statements were intended to draw attention to broader immigration issues. "We're creating a story, meaning we're creating the American media focusing on it," he said, justifying his rhetoric as a means to highlight what he viewed as underreported problems with immigration policy.

This acknowledgment—that the allegations were less about factual accuracy and more about controlling the narrative—drew widespread condemnation. Critics argued that it was irresponsible and dangerous for a public figure to make inflammatory claims without evidence, particularly when those claims targeted vulnerable communities. The controversy also raised ethical questions about the use of misinformation in political discourse.

The fallout from the Springfield allegations was significant, both for JD's reputation and for the broader political climate. While his base largely stood by him, seeing his comments as a bold challenge to political correctness and media bias, others viewed the incident as a troubling example of divisive rhetoric. Advocacy groups and local leaders called for greater accountability, arguing that such unsubstantiated claims endangered communities and undermined public trust.

Despite the criticism, JD remained unapologetic. He framed the controversy as part of his broader fight against what he described as the failures of the Biden administration's immigration policies. By linking the allegations to larger themes of border security and resource allocation, he sought to shift the focus from the specifics of the claims to the perceived inadequacies of federal governance.

A Polarizing Figure

The Springfield controversy encapsulated many of the qualities that made JD a polarizing figure in American politics. His willingness to amplify unverified claims, even in the face of widespread criticism, demonstrated his commitment to a confrontational style of politics. For his supporters, this approach made him a fearless advocate for their concerns. For his detractors, it marked him as a reckless and divisive figure willing to sacrifice truth for political gain.

In the months that followed, the incident became a defining moment in JD's career, highlighting both the strengths and the pitfalls of his political strategy. It underscored the risks of prioritizing attention-grabbing rhetoric over measured discourse and raised enduring questions about the role of truth in an increasingly polarized political landscape. As JD continued his rise, the Springfield controversy remained a stark reminder of the complexities and consequences of wielding populist rhetoric in the digital age.

CHAPTER 38

____

Chapter: The Vice Presidential Debate of 2024

The Vice Presidential Debate of 2024, held on October 1 at the CBS Broadcast Center in New York City, marked a pivotal moment in the heated race for the White House. Moderated by Margaret Brennan and Norah O'Donnell, the event showcased a fierce exchange of ideas between Republican vice presidential candidate JDand Democratic vice presidential nominee Tim Walz. Both candidates faced the task of defending their respective running mates' policies and addressing the pressing concerns of the nation.

The debate almost didn't happen. Following President Biden's withdrawal from the race in July 2024, Vice President Kamala Harris launched her own presidential campaign, raising doubts about the debate's viability. JD, initially annoyed at losing the chance to debate Harris, soon shifted his focus to Walz, who had recently been chosen as Harris's running mate. Walz expressed enthusiasm about the opportunity, stating his willingness to engage with JD on the issues.

CBS proposed four dates for the debate, eventually settling on October 1. Walz agreed to the date immediately, and JD followed suit the next day. As preparations intensified, Republican Representative Tom Emmer took on the role of Walz in JD's practice sessions, while Transportation Secretary Pete Buttigieg played JD in Walz's rehearsals.

The debate lasted 90 minutes, featuring a structured format that left little room for candidate interaction beyond their responses to the moderators' questions. Unlike earlier debates in 2024, both candidates' microphones remained on while the other spoke, though CBS retained the right to mute them if necessary. Each candidate presented their closing arguments sequentially, with Walz going first, followed by JD

Policy Debates and Heated Exchanges

The economy was a central theme of the debate. Walz championed Harris's proposals to reduce costs for housing and prescription drugs, presenting them as solutions to the nation's economic struggles. JD countered that Harris's plans "sound pretty good" but criticized her for not implementing them during her tenure as vice president. He placed the blame for current economic woes squarely on Harris and emphasized that more voters trusted Donald Trump's economic leadership.

Abortion policy became another flashpoint. Walz invoked the tragic case of Amber Thurman, a woman who died following complications from a medical abortion, arguing that restrictive abortion laws had fatal consequences. JD expressed agreement with Walz's concern, stating, "Amber Thurman should still be alive," while clarifying that he did not support a national abortion ban, despite previous support for a "minimum national standard" during his Senate campaign.

On climate change, the candidates presented starkly different visions. JD declared the United States the "cleanest economy in the entire world," a claim later disputed by fact-checkers. He argued for reshoring manufacturing and expanding nuclear energy to address climate change while criticizing Harris for insufficient investment in natural gas. Walz, in turn, acknowledged the reality of climate change and emphasized the importance of reducing environmental impact. He highlighted achievements under the Bipartisan Infrastructure Law and pointed to record-high natural gas production.

Immigration policies also fueled fiery exchanges. JD reiterated Trump's campaign pledge for a large-scale deportation plan, emphasizing the need to deport "about a million" immigrants who had committed crimes beyond illegal entry. He blamed Harris for what he termed a "wide-open southern border." Walz defended Harris's record as California's attorney general and criticized Trump for failing to deliver on his 2016 promises, such as building a border wall funded by Mexico. Walz also noted Trump's role in derailing the bipartisan Secure the Border Act in 2023, which aimed to enhance border security.

On the 2020 election and January 6, JD refused to explicitly acknowledge Trump's loss, stating, "Tim, I'm focused on the future." Walz described JD's response as "a damning non-answer" and accused him of downplaying the severity of the Capitol attack. JD, in turn, shifted the discussion to allegations of social media censorship, highlighting what he saw as a lack of free speech in the digital age.

CBS decided against real-time fact-checking during the debate, opting instead to provide analysis after the event. However, a contentious moment arose when JD faced scrutiny for his previous comments about Haitian immigrants in Springfield, Ohio. He objected to the moderators' reference to his disputed claims, arguing that the debate rules precluded fact-checking. JD maintained that federal decisions on protected status for immigrants did not align with the concerns of local residents, but his microphone was muted as he continued to speak.

Public Response and Media Coverage

The debate drew significant public attention, with Nielsen Media Research reporting 43 million viewers across CBS and affiliated networks. While viewership fell short of the 57 million who watched the 2020 vice presidential debate, the event generated widespread discussion. Analysts noted that Walz spoke for a slightly longer duration than JD, with CNN clocking his speaking time at approximately 40 minutes and 42 seconds compared to JD's 38 minutes and 59 seconds.

Critics and supporters alike dissected the candidates' performances. JD's comments on immigration and his handling of the 2020 election allegations drew praise from his base for their combative tone but attracted criticism for their lack of specificity. Walz, on the other hand, was lauded for his measured responses and his ability to pivot to Harris's accomplishments, though some argued that his performance lacked the forcefulness needed to counter JD's direct style.

The vice presidential debate became a defining moment in the 2024 campaign. It highlighted the stark ideological divide between the candidates and underscored the broader contrasts between the Trump and Harris tickets. For JD, the debate reinforced his reputation as a sharp and unapologetic defender of Trump's policies, willing to tackle contentious issues head-on. For Walz, the event provided an opportunity to present Harris's platform as a practical and compassionate alternative, even as he faced the challenge of countering JD's aggressive rhetoric.

As the campaign moved forward, the debate served as a microcosm of the broader political landscape, marked by sharp divisions on policy, leadership, and the future direction of the United States. For voters, it was a moment to assess the candidates not just as vice presidential contenders but as potential leaders poised to shape the nation's destiny.

Reception of the 2024 Vice Presidential Debate

The 2024 vice presidential debate between JD and Tim Walz received widespread attention, with political pundits and the general public closely analyzing the performances. While polls and commentary highlighted a balanced and civil exchange, JD emerged as the slight favorite in several assessments, solidifying his role as a formidable contender in the election.

Media outlets and polling organizations reflected a competitive outcome. According to CNN, 51% of viewers believed JD had won, compared to 49% for Walz. CBS's flash poll showed a narrower margin, with 42% favoring JD, 41% favoring Walz, and 17% considering it a tie. Politico/Focaldata's poll declared the debate a dead heat at 50% each, reflecting the sharp polarization of the electorate. Notably, 88% of viewers in the CBS/YouGov poll described the tone of the debate as "generally positive," a marked contrast to the often combative nature of the presidential debates.

JD's debate performance was lauded by several leading media outlets. The New York Times described it as "one of the best debating performances by a Republican nominee for president or vice president in recent memory," praising his ability to effectively champion Trump's record while drawing on his personal biography to connect with viewers. Similarly, Politico commended JD for delivering a sharp critique of the Biden-Harris administration while tactfully distancing himself from some of his more controversial past remarks about women and immigrants.

The Financial Times and USA Today also highlighted JD's composure and clarity, noting that his middle-class background and military service narrative resonated strongly with voters. The Wall Street Journal underscored his ability to navigate the fine line between defending Trump's policies and presenting himself as an independent thinker with fresh ideas for the nation.

One of the defining characteristics of the debate was its civility and policy-focused discussion. Both JD and Walz avoided personal attacks, opting instead to address pressing national issues like the economy, immigration, and climate change. The Washington Post and Reuters praised both candidates for maintaining a high level of decorum, with The Post calling it "a debate Americans could watch without cringing."

The event ended on a collegial note. After their closing statements, JD and Walz were seen chatting amicably and introducing their spouses to one another. This moment of mutual respect underscored the professionalism of the debate and set it apart from the often acrimonious exchanges in modern political discourse.

Challenges and Criticism

While JD received accolades for his performance, he was not without his detractors. Some critics noted his reluctance to acknowledge Trump's 2020 election loss, an omission Politico referred to as "a missed opportunity to broaden his appeal to undecided voters." Fact-checkers also questioned his claim that the United States is the "cleanest economy in the world," pointing out inaccuracies in his statement.

Still, JD's focus on policy and his ability to draw a stark contrast between Trump's vision and the Biden-Harris administration's record bolstered his standing among Republican voters. His appeal to middle-class Americans, rooted in his personal story of overcoming hardship, further enhanced his relatability and credibility.

The vice presidential debate was a turning point in the 2024 election, showcasing JDas a capable and compelling candidate. His strong performance, combined with his ability to maintain civility and focus on policy, helped him solidify his position in the race. The event also demonstrated that even in a highly polarized political environment, respectful and substantive debate remains possible, leaving an indelible mark on the campaign narrative.

CHAPTER 39

Balancing Public and Private

In the wake of his election to the U.S. Senate, JD Vance found himself navigating the uncharted waters of balancing a demanding public career with the responsibilities of family life. Amid the glare of national attention, JD remained anchored by his relationship with his wife, Usha, and their three children. The challenges of reconciling his roles as a senator and a family man became a defining aspect of his post-election journey.

Usha, whom JD met during their time at Yale Law School, has been a steady and unwavering presence in his life. A legal professional in her own right, Usha brings her own sense of discipline and focus to their partnership, a dynamic that has often helped JD navigate the unpredictable nature of politics. "She's the better half in every sense of the word," JD has said, acknowledging her ability to ground him during moments of stress. Usha's support extends beyond the personal, as she often provides counsel on navigating complex political situations, blending her legal expertise with her understanding of JD's values.

Despite their busy schedules, JD and Usha have made it a priority to preserve family routines, seeing them as a sanctuary amid the chaos of public life. Weekend mornings are often reserved for family breakfasts, where they put away their phones and focus on their children. "No matter what's happening in Washington, pancakes with the kids remind me why I do this work," JD remarked in an interview. These small moments, though seemingly mundane, serve as a vital reminder of the life they've built together.

Parenting three young children while serving in the Senate is no small feat. JD has spoken candidly about the guilt that comes with missing milestones or being away during critical family moments. He has described the bittersweet feeling of kissing his kids goodbye before heading to the airport on Monday mornings, knowing he won't see them again until the weekend. "You never stop wondering if you're doing enough as a dad," he admitted, a sentiment echoed by many working parents.

To mitigate the strain of his frequent absences, JD and Usha have implemented creative strategies to stay connected as a family. Video calls have become a staple of their routine, with JD often reading bedtime stories to his children over Zoom. "Even if I'm in D.C., I want them to know I'm still part of their day," he explained. These moments, though virtual, help maintain a sense of presence and continuity in their lives.

For Usha, managing the household while JD is away has required resilience and adaptability. Friends describe her as fiercely protective of their family's privacy, shielding their children from the intense scrutiny that comes with public life. At the same time, she encourages JD to involve their kids in his work in meaningful ways. Family visits to Washington, D.C., have become an opportunity for the children to see their father in action, attending events and even sitting in on a Senate hearing. "I want them to understand that their dad's job is about helping people," Usha has said, emphasizing the importance of framing JD's work in a positive light.

The demands of public life have also tested JD and Usha's marriage in unexpected ways. The constant travel, long hours, and public scrutiny can strain even the strongest relationships, but the couple has leaned on open communication and mutual respect to navigate these challenges. JD credits Usha's ability to call him out when he gets caught up in the whirlwind of politics, reminding him to prioritize what truly matters. "She keeps me honest," he said, reflecting on the importance of having a partner who isn't afraid to hold him accountable.

As JD continues to balance his roles as a senator and a family man, he remains acutely aware of the example he's setting for his children. He often reflects on the lessons he learned from his grandparents, Mamaw and Papaw, and the values of loyalty and resilience they instilled in him. These principles, he hopes, will guide his own children as they grow up in a world vastly different from the one he knew in Middletown, Ohio.

In the end, JD views the balancing act of public and private life not as a burden but as a responsibility. "My family is my anchor," he says. "They remind me that the work I do isn't just about politics—it's about building a future they can be proud of." It's a delicate equilibrium, but for JD, the effort is more than worth it.

Made in United States
Orlando, FL
03 February 2025